Literacy in Historical Perspective

Edited by Daniel P. Resnick

WASHINGTON LIBRARY OF CONGRESS 1983

Library of Congress Cataloging in Publication Data
Main entry under title:

Literacy in historical perspective.

Eight papers commissioned for a conference held at the Library of Congress in July 1980, which was sponsored by the Center for the Book and the National Institute of Education.
Includes bibliographical references.
Supt. of Docs. no.: LC 1.2: L71
1. Literacy—History—Congresses. I. Resnick, Daniel Philip. II. Center for the Book. III. National Institute of Education (U.S.)
LC149.L499   1983   302.2′09   82-600295
ISBN O-8444-0410-1

For sale by the Superintendent of Documents,
U.S. Government Printing Office
Washington, D.C. 20402

Contents

Preface

In July 1980 the Center for the Book in the Library of Congress and the U.S. National Institute of Education sponsored a conference entitled "Literacy in Historical Perspective." Its purpose was to bring historians and educators together with government officials to learn about literacy research already in progress and to discuss research that was needed. A description of the conference and list of the participants is found in the Library of Congress *Information Bulletin,* October 10, 1980. The Center for the Book is pleased to present eight of the papers commissioned for that meeting in this volume. Special thanks go to the National Institute of Education for its funding and to the other conference organizers: Ramsey Selden, literacy team leader at the NIE when the meeting was held, and Daniel P. Resnick, professor of history at Carnegie-Mellon University and editor of this book.

Established in 1977 by Librarian of Congress Daniel J. Boorstin, the Center for the Book is a national catalyst for promoting books, reading, and the printed word. By bringing together members of the book, educational, and business communities for symposia and projects, it strives to improve communication among all those who care about books and reading. Its publications, which deal with a wide range of subjects, enable the center to reach a broader audience. Subjects of previous publications include reading and reading promotion; the past, present, and future role of the book in society; television and reading; and the international role of the book. While the Library of Congress provides administrative support, the center's program is financed primarily by tax-deductible contributions from generous individuals and organizations. Further information is available from the Center for the Book, Library of Congress, Washington, D.C. 20540.

John Y. Cole
Executive Director
The Center for the Book

Spreading the Word: An Introduction

by Daniel P. Resnick

Daniel P. Resnick is professor of history at Carnegie-Mellon University, a member of the Program in Applied History and Social Science, and the principal organizer of the conference at which these papers were presented. He is currently at work, with Lauren B. Resnick, on a book on testing and standards in public education. Professor Resnick has published articles on changing historical standards for literacy, on selection in education, and on various aspects of testing.

Of all the ways employed by the human spirit to demonstrate and memorialize its playfulness, its participation in communities, and its search for knowledge, writing is the most complex. Like the more primary modes of communication—song, dance, and gesture, which it has succeeded but not replaced—the written word is both expressive and functional, belonging to the world of art and of everyday life. Its practice has given form to our civilization, to recreation, commerce, politics, and science.

Writing and the collateral skill of reading—decoding and finding meaning in text—are no more than five thousand years old, a gift to the Western world from ancient Near Eastern and Aegean civilizations. Nothing in the nature of reading and writing required that it be the skill of a chosen few. Indeed, the phonetic alphabet to which we have been heir from these ancient sources faithfully transcribed the spoken tongue, creating a bridge to the oral tradition of preliterate cultures.

Yet for most of history, reading and writing have been the monopoly of a small elite who served the religious and secular authority. But because the art of fashioning letters and deciphering their meaning lay within the reach of nearly all, the barriers that surrounded access to the printed word were destined to fall.

Within the Western world, the spread of literacy was assured, even before the revolution of printing at the end of the fifteenth century, by three centuries of growing reliance in public life on written records rather than oral testimony. As the surviving sources from the period of the twelfth to the fifteenth centuries indicate, state taxation and justice, like commerce, property law, and a variety of Church transactions, were changing in ways that favored the use of more and more written records. This movement touched even the most isolated of rural communities, although in different ways and with varying intensity.

As previously nonliterate groups joined the ranks of those who could read, the definition of the literate person began to change. In the twelfth century, *clericus* and *litteratus* still had very similar meanings—to be literate was to be learned in Latin—a privilege still held almost exclusively by the clergy. By the end of the fifteenth century, however, *litteratus* and *clericus* were no longer confounded, and literacy was no longer monopolized by the clergy.[1]

This coming into being of a public that could read was a necessary precursor to the adoption of the technology of the printing press, for it provided what we would call a growing market. The first products of the new printing technology at the end of the fifteenth century were, of course, the very same kinds of texts that were previously circulated in manuscript form, for which there was a known demand. These were the religious works—prayers, psalters, catechisms, biblical stories, saints' lives, and the like.

Among the Protestant reformers of the sixteenth century, Martin Luther, in particular, was quick to recognize the potential of printing for spreading the divine word. In the *Little Catechism* he created a text that could serve for instruction in the Christian religion. The kind of literacy he desired was one that would bond the reader closely to the tenets of Luther's own beliefs—a literacy that would promote tradition, family values, and faith. It was a literacy that could be taught in the home and would be supported by the liturgy of the church.

Some remarkable results were recorded in the literacy movements that flowed from Lutheranism. The best documented of these, for the present, is the success of Swedish reading instruction in the seventeenth and eighteenth centuries. Through the *Little Catechism*, reading instruction was given in the home, with the reinforcement of church assemblies and regular visits by religious authorities. When the priest visited homes in a parish, he asked the members of a family to read and answer questions about various parts of the *Little Catechism*. The priest's judgments about the reader's ability to read and answer questions has been recorded in a number of registers for different parishes.[2]

These registers are evidence of the first successful literacy crusade in the modern West, carried out with very traditional materials. The success rate, based on criteria we shall discuss shortly, compares very favorably with the results that have been reported from Cuba, Nicaragua, and China, to name the more revolutionary experiments of our own century. In Sweden, between 1645 and 1714, the literacy rates for males increased in the parishes of one region from 50 to 98 percent.

But there are many different kinds and levels of literacy—a fact that may be overlooked when we apply the term *literate* to different populations in different settings.[3] The literacy demanded of those who used the *Little Catechism* was of a very simple kind. Readers were given a text that was familiar to them from recitation and asked to recite it aloud. The questions that were then asked required answers that summarized the material or simply repeated it. There was no invitation to speculate on its various possible meanings.

Psychologists and reading specialists acknowledge a very broad spread in the kinds of capabilities that readers possess. At one end of the spectrum lies the literal rendering of the most familiar kinds of material and at the other, a capacity to make inferences from written text and to generalize and transfer what has been learned to other settings. This description of the varied skills and capabilities that readers may possess corresponds with certain typologies and hierarchies that have been developed by psychologists to describe the stages of reasoning ability. In some of these models, it is writing that introduces a stage of logical thinking that is not possible in cultures with only an oral tradition.[4] Even so, the growth of modern literacy in the West must be described in terms of not simply a rise in the capabilities of the reader and writer, but also the increasing access to all levels of skill by ever larger portions of the public.

Since written communication has been central to the way we have defined ourselves as a civilization, it has appeared on the research agenda of almost all of our disciplines. Psychologists have been concerned with the way written material is processed by the reader, and rhetoricians with the ways in which persuasion proceeds through written discourse. Economists have investigated the benefits and costs of investment in education, while sociologists have paid particular attention to socialization and the effects of schooling. No single discipline has monopolized this study.

3

Historians and anthropologists, however, have had the broadest concern with the social experience of literacy and its meaning. The former have examined the growth of books and newspapers, the appearance of libraries, the emergence of mass public schooling, and the evidence for literacy presented by the ability to sign.[5] The latter have tried to look at the effects of access to reading and writing on the cognitive capabilities of subgroups within different cultures and in a broader way at the relationship of oral traditions and literate culture.[6]

This research on literacy in other societies and settings may be helpful to participants in the current debate over American literacy goals. There is great public concern today over the effectiveness of our schooling, the reading tastes of our public, and the kinds of investments that ought to be made to raise standards. Perhaps because of this controversy, there is considerable interest in the range of questions to which historians and anthropologists have increasingly directed their attention. What has been responsible for the spread of literacy in the past? What abilities have characterized the literate? What environments have promoted literacy most effectively and in what ways? How has the ability to read and write affected life goals, mobility, and the attitude toward traditional values?

A group of historians and anthropologists, along with critics from a number of disciplines, were brought together by the Center for the Book at the Library of Congress on July 14–15, 1980, to deal with these questions. The papers they produced were excellent statements of what is currently known about certain aspects of the spread of literacy in the medieval and modern periods. Selected contributions have been revised for publication in this volume.

In the chapters that follow, six historians and one anthropologist look at the relationship between literacy demand and environment in particular national settings over the past seven centuries. The sources of demand for literacy in England are explored before the introduction of the printing press, and the spread of literacy in England and New England is traced in the centuries that follow. China and Russia are examined during the prerevolutionary years when proposals for bringing basic literacy to the mass of the population were first introduced. The question is then posed of how we may best proceed to foster basic literacy among minorities in American urban centers today.

The concluding essay reviews seminal work in other fields or subdisciplines that has influenced the thinking of many of our contributors.

Those who have shared their ideas with one another in these pages and in the halls of the Library of Congress gained a strong sense of the relevance of their research for the priorities of our nation in raising levels of literacy, training, and communication. For their support of our endeavors, we would like to express our appreciation to the National Institute of Education and its literacy project leader, Ramsey Selden; the Center for the Book in the Library of Congress; and the Rockefeller Foundation, which, at Carnegie-Mellon University, has underwritten many historical investigations that bear on current public policy.

Notes

1. For an excellent discussion of these developments, see M. T. Clanchy, *From Memory to Written Record: England, 1066–1307* (Cambridge, Mass.: Harvard University Press, 1979), esp. Ch. 7.

2. Egil Johansson, "Literacy Studies in Sweden: Some Examples," in *Literacy and Society in a Historical Perspective: A Conference Report,* ed. E. Johansson, Educational Reports Umea (Umea, Sweden: Umea University and School of Education, 1973).

3. Daniel P. Resnick and Lauren B. Resnick, "The Nature of Literacy: An Historical Exploration," *Harvard Educational Review* 47, no. 3 (August 1977): 370–85.

4. P. Greenfield and J. Bruner, "Culture and Cognitive Growth," *International Journal of Psychology* 1 (1966): 89–107; P. Greenfield, "Oral or Written Language: The Consequences for Cognitive Development in Africa, the United States and England," *Language and Speech* 15 (1972): 169–78; D. Olson, "From Utterance to Text: The Bias of Language in Speech and Writing," *Harvard Educational Review* 47 (1977): 257–81; S. Scribner and M. Cole, "Literacy Without Schooling:

Testing for Intellectual Effects," *Harvard Educational Review* 48, no. 4 (November 1978): 448–61.

5. An extended bibliography of such work appears in Harvey Graff, *Literacy in History: An Interdisciplinary Research Bibliography* (New York: Greenwood Press, 1981). For the use of signatures as an index of ability to read in seventeenth- and eighteenth-century England, see Roger S. Schofield, "The Measurement of Literacy in Pre-Industrial England," in *Literacy in Traditional Societies,* ed. Jack R. Goody (Cambridge, Eng.: Cambridge University Press, 1968), 311–25. The uses of signatures for retrospective literacy assessment in France are discussed in François Furet and Vladimir Sachs, "La Croissance de l'alphabétisation en France (XVIIIe–XIXe siecles)," *Annales: Economies, Sociétés, Civilisations* 29 (1974): 714–37; François Furet and Jacques Ozouf, *Lire et Ecrire* (Paris: Editions de Minuit, 1977) vol. I, 19–28.

6. On the relationship of literacy to oral traditions, see Jack Goody, *The Domestication of the Savage Mind* (Cambridge, Eng.: Cambridge University Press, 1977).

Looking Back from
the Invention of Printing

by Michael T. Clanchy

Michael T. Clanchy is reader in medieval history at the University of Glasgow. He has been at work for several years on a study of how readership grew and became secularized in the last few centuries before the introduction of the printing press in England.

Extending the argument presented in From Memory to Written Record: England, 1066–1307 *(Cambridge, Mass.: Harvard University Press, 1979), Dr. Clanchy says that our modern view of literacy as public and useful has its roots before the introduction of the printing press in high medieval civil administration and public law.*

The invention of printing with movable type in Europe in the middle of the fifteenth century is commonly seen as the starting point of a new age. Modern and progressive times begin with printing; the period preceding it is obscurantist and medieval. Without printing, literacy could never have advanced, and our modern world would have been inconceivable. In this way of thinking, the invention of printing is associated with the Renaissance, which revived classical learning, and the Reformation, which brought knowledge to the people. The thousand years of European history between 450 and 1450 then became a negative time, the Middle Ages, sandwiched between the classical world of antiquity and the modern world of progress. This frame of thought fails to put the invention of printing, and the literate culture which produced it, into a sufficiently long historical perspective. Historians tend to overdramatize and to present the period in which they specialize—whatever it is—as the starting point of a new age. The history of medieval literacy has suffered from this. For example, Lucien Febvre and Henri-Jean Martin entitled their work on the effects of printing *L'Apparition du Livre* (translated as *The Coming of the Book*), and Margaret B. Stillwell entitled hers *The Beginning of the World of Books, 1450 to 1470.*[1] These are excellent

7

works, but their titles are misleading, since the book made its appearance in the fourth century, not in the fifteenth, and beginning a world of books was the work of medieval monks and not of printers.

Printing and Medieval Tradition

Instead of viewing printing as the starting point of a new age, I want to look at it as the endpoint or culmination of a millennium. Writing was of extraordinary importance in medieval culture; otherwise printing would not have been invented.[2] To the unanswerable question "Why was printing invented in Europe in the 1450s?" I would hypothesize that Western Europe had by that time achieved a more vigorous literate culture than any previous civilization in the world including China. The elements of that literate culture are the subject of this paper. Historians of literacy have tended to concentrate on its extension to the masses and its measurement by minimal but uniform tests (particularly the ability to sign one's name) in the last two or three centuries. But it is as important to explain how literacy first established itself and became sufficiently vigorous to sustain the mass production of printing. Medieval intellectuals were aware that they were dwarfs who stood on the shoulders of giants (the prophets of the Old Testament and the sages of Greece and Rome) and thus saw further than their forbears.[3] We modern educators on the other hand are less ready to acknowledge that we in our turn stand on the shoulders of the monks and schoolmen of the Middle Ages who pioneered books. The immediate consequence of printing was to make medieval books more widely available. Marshall McLuhan's epigram, "the sixteenth and seventeenth centuries saw more of the Middle Ages than had ever been available to anybody in the Middle Ages," needs stressing.[4] Assessments vary, but at least three-quarters of all books printed before 1500 were in Latin and most books printed in the next century were by medieval or ancient authors.[5] While in some areas of experience printing marked a new start, in others it reinforced medieval ways of thinking because it caused them to be more uniformly diffused.[6]

In order to show how printing grew out of the medieval environment, I will concentrate on what Gutenberg of Mainz, the inventor of European printing, aimed to achieve. This is a contentious subject, however, because the invention of printing is not well documented. Its pioneers were not the academics and authors who were to benefit from it, but technologists and businessmen for whom it was an industrial venture. Gutenberg was a goldsmith and his partner, Fust, was a lawyer. The first dated printed book, the Psalter of 1457, bears the names of Fust and Schoeffer, who was the type designer. Such men, like the largely anonymous craftsmen who built the medieval cathedrals, tended to be secretive and practical. They were not accustomed to exposing their thoughts for posterity in the way monks and academics did. Consequently the earliest evidence about printing, as about so many medieval developments, can only be glimpsed through the formal records of lawsuits. Gutenberg's colleagues were disappointed with him and sued him for failing to produce the goods. How had he disappointed them? The most attractive hypothesis is that Gutenberg was a perfectionist who intended to produce a perfect book, whereas his colleagues demanded a more immediate return on their investment.[7]

The problem Gutenberg faced was to produce something as good as even the average medieval book. Although block-books (such as the woodcut *Biblia Pauperum*) were probably produced earlier than Gutenberg's invention, they were far inferior in appearance to books written by scribes and were therefore not a solution to his problems.[8] Gutenberg could not hope to surpass the best medieval books, for no books have ever surpassed in quality of production such works as the Book of Kells, the Winchester Bible, and the Très Riches Heures du Duc de Berry. Medieval manuscript books are among the greatest works of art in the world. Their texts are generally elegant and ordered, written with highly controlled regularity of penmanship, and they are embellished with colored inks to clarify the text for the reader and to please the eye. Very few, of course, are as fine as the lavish illuminated manuscripts mentioned above, which were made for princes both religious and secular, but, conversely, really badly written manuscripts are even more unusual. (Incompetent work is a subject which has not yet attracted the systematic attention of students of medieval paleography and illumination.) The manuscript books of Gutenberg's time were not therefore primitive precursors of printed books. On the contrary, they presented an image of perfection, encapsulating a thousand years of experience. That fact is demonstrated here in the Library of Congress by the manuscript Giant Bible of Mainz, which emanates from the same time and place as the earliest printing.[9] Gutenberg likewise seems to have thought that his books must be as perfect as possible if he were to win a market for them.

The kind of market resistance Gutenberg may have feared is revealed in the denunciation of printed books by Johannes Trithemius, abbot of Sponheim, in 1492: "If writing is put on to parchment it can last for a thousand years, but how long will printing on something paper last? At the most a paper book could last for two hundred years." [10] In fact Trithemius was unduly pessimistic; he had refused to admit the competitive standards set by Gutenberg, as the best printed books have survived the centuries. Furthermore Trithemius himself used the printing press to disseminate his views, and he was in fact one of the pioneers of publishing. [11] Nevertheless the contrast made by Trithemius between traditional manuscripts and printed books does illustrate a fundamental difference between medieval and modern attitudes to technology. Medieval monks took a long view of time, because they lived under God's eternal providence and wrote their books as an act of worship and a sacred charge for posterity. Modern technology, on the other hand, of which printing was the forerunner, takes a very short view, because it responds to a mass demand in the present regardless of the consequences. In the passage cited above, Trithemius sees printing as an essentially superficial process (the words are superimposed on frail paper), whereas the medieval scribe incised the words into the parchment with his pen. The act of writing was often likened by monks to ploughing the fields: "The pages are ploughed by the divine letters and the seed of God's word is planted in the parchment, which ripens into crops of completed books (*libri perfecti*)." [12] Medieval scribal culture demanded that printing, unlike other technologies, should start fully developed because printers too had to produce *libri perfecti*.

The Earliest Printing

What has survived of early printing is partly a matter of chance, and the chronology is imprecise. Even so, enough has now been established by scholars to make a pattern discernible. Of particular significance are the earliest works of all, because these indicate the types of medieval writing which Gutenberg and his associates thought could best be exploited by printing. Later printers profited from their experience, whereas they—like the Portuguese navigators who were their contemporaries—had to venture into uncharted seas. The records of these first voyages into the printing market are therefore peculiarly valuable. The works of the first two decades of printing (1450–70) have been conveniently listed by Margaret B. Stillwell. I will narrow the list even further and consider the thirty-nine pieces of printing which are ascribed to the first decade ending in 1460. When analysed by function these pieces fall into three main categories, with a fourth category on the periphery:

(1) Sacred Literacy. In pride of place stand the Latin Bibles and prayer books (eleven items), which include the largest and most magnificent works: the 42-line Bible (the first printed book), the Psalter of 1457 (the first dated printed book), and the 36-line Bible.[13] I would describe the common factor of function in these works as "Sacred Literacy": these were the principal texts in the church's liturgy, with the books of the Latin vulgate Bible (the translation of St. Jerome done in the late fourth century) as their foundation.

(2) Learned Literacy. In the second category I place seven pieces of Donatus, the basic Latin grammar, which (like the vulgate Bible) had been in use since the late fourth century.[14] In this category likewise I place four scholastic works (three of them dating from the thirteenth century, including a piece of Aquinas) and one medical calendar.[15] These twelve items I would describe as providing for "Learned Literacy": the tradition of Latin learning which had taken shape in the late Roman Empire and developed through the Twelfth-Century Renaissance into the *summae* of the schoolmen. As Latin teachers never wearied of repeating, grammar was the basis of all this learning, and it is therefore appropriate that Donatus should have been so frequently printed at the beginning.

(3) Bureaucratic Literacy. In the third category I place four indulgence certificates issued in the name of Pope Nicholas V (1447–55) for the crusade, two papal bulls (one translated into German) likewise concerning the crusade, and five pieces (mainly papal bulls) concerning canon law.[16] These eleven items are products of the development of papal authority since the twelfth century. This was characterized by the issue of thousands—and by the fourteenth century of hundreds of thousands—of papal letters or *decreta* which formed the basis of the canon law. Printing was well suited to the proliferation of such documents as indulgence certificates, as they were common form apart from the blanks which could be left for the date and the beneficiary's name.[17] (The earliest dated printing from England by Caxton is likewise an indulgence certificate from 1476.[18]) This use of printing I would describe as catering for practical or "Bureaucratic Literacy." This was concerned not with books as such but with documents, and it had its medieval origins not in the fourth century but in the twelfth- and thirteenth-century growth of bureaucracy all across Western Europe.

(4) Vernacular Literacy. Finally, five of the thirty-nine earliest pieces of printing are directed exclusively at German readers instead of Latin. Two of these have death and the last judgment as their subject, and the other three are likewise concerned with prognostication as they are forms of calendars.[19] I would describe the common factor in these pieces as "Vernacular Literacy": works which appealed to a wider public than the elite of Latin readers. The long-term future of education lay of course with the vernacular languages. Nevertheless, judged by early printing, their place was still peripheral. Vernacular works appealed to a relatively wide public within a particular region, but against this had to be set the fact that they were restricted to a particular language area. Latin on the other hand provided an international market, and it still retained unique prestige. As the language of literacy for a millennium and more, it had proved to be the hardiest of perennials. To be literate ideally meant to be learned in Latin in the fifteenth century as much as it had in the fifth or in the days of Cicero.[20]

As has often been pointed out, neither in their appearance nor in their content do these earliest pieces of printing differ from manuscripts. The printers aimed to imitate manuscripts as closely as possible. This presented the first type designers with unusual problems, as they had to provide type for numerous letter forms and for the abbreviations used by medieval scribes.[21] The first "sacred" books were printed in various fonts of Gothic type (the formal book hand of manuscripts), whereas such "bureaucratic" documents as indulgence certificates imitated the cursive hands of chanceries. Whether manuscript or print, each script had to appear in its appropriate form in order to be valid. Gutenberg would not have dreamed of altering the "sacred page" of scripture, or the traditional transmission of literacy in imprints of Donatus; still less would it have been wise to tamper with the routines of papal bureaucracy. The most challenging problem was to reproduce in print the variety of color in medieval manuscripts. As has already been suggested, Gutenberg seems to have been determined to do this, whereas his colleagues Fust and Schoeffer were satisfied with a little less.[22] In the first printed book, the 42-line Bible, the rubrication and border illumination was done by hand. Yet even Fust and Schoeffer were perfectionists by later standards, as the Psalter they produced in 1457 was printed in three colors (black, red, and blue), and it even has printed calligraphic ornament.[23] What it lacks, which Gutenberg perhaps aspired to, are colored images in the margins likewise produced by print. Gutenberg succeeded in automating the scribe but not the artist.

Looking Back at Sacred Literacy

By looking back from the earliest evidence of printing, we discern across the medieval centuries those elements in the development of writing which made the printed book possible. The most fundamental creation of all was the book itself. In the ancient world the scroll was the usual format of writing. The book or codex format, comprising pages which are turned over, was known to the Romans but its use was uncommon and secondary to scrolls. The early Christians seem to have positively favored the book format, because it distinguished their scriptures from those of the Jews and pagans.[24] They also first developed the abbreviations so characteristic of medieval and early printed texts. Christianity likewise seems to have been responsible for the changeover from papyrus to parchment as the commonest writing material. This change cannot be explained in utilitarian terms, since papyrus is in fact as resilient as parchment. However, like the scroll format, papyrus may have been too closely associated in the minds of early Christians with the pagan lore of antiquity, which they were determined to supersede. Christianity can thus be said to have invented the parchment book, whose official baptism is marked in 332 A.D. by the Emperor Constantine's order for vellum Bibles in the principal churches.

By the seventh century, Christian manuscripts were distinguished from all others not only by the book format but by their being illuminated.[25] Although some writings in the pagan Mediterranean world had colored illustrations,[26] these are different in character from medieval illuminated manuscripts. The difference is that in medieval manuscripts individual letters, as distinct from pages or subjects, are embellished with precious paints and often with images as well: these are not illustrations but illuminations. The effect of illuminations was to make books both awesome and attractive. The modern utilitarian reader will say that such illumination is unnecessary and indeed inappropriate in printed books, but that is wisdom after the event. The monks of the seventh century who pioneered illumination in such sublime works as the Book of Kells and the Lindisfarne Gospels evidently thought it essential. They were writing the *sacra pagina,* the "sacred page" of the scripture, in the expression of which no trouble or expense could be too great.[27] Monastic scribes were not hireling scriveners, like the slave writers of the ancient world, but the Lord's shepherds who enfolded the divine words in the interface of their designs. Their work fills the modern viewer with wonder at its craftsmanship and that is the right reaction, because illumination was intended to be wonder-working. The earliest Irish manuscript with decorated letters, the *Cathach* (the "Battler") of St. Columba (dating from about 600 A.D.), was so called because it was carried in battle as a talisman.[28] The Lindisfarne Gospels and other great liturgical books were similarly treated as holy relics.

Monastic illumination of manuscripts gave to writings a force and prestige which was unprecedented. Throughout the millennium of Western monasticism (500–1500 A.D.), the rich founded monasteries so that monks might pray and worship on their behalf. The monks displayed the fruit of their labors to their patrons in their churches and other works of art, particularly in their books. When with growing prosperity from about 1250 onwards the demand for individual prayer reached down to the middle class of knights and burgesses, they began to want wonder-working books of their own.[29] They could not afford to buy a chantry chapel or a jeweled reliquary, but a small illuminated manuscript came within their means as the first step towards the purchase of paradise. Ladies in particular took to reciting the Latin Psalter and treasuring illuminated books of hours. In fifteenth-century depictions of the Annunication, Mary is often shown seated in a sunlit bower with an open book of hours on her lap or displayed on a lectern.[30] Likewise she is sometimes depicted with the child Jesus on her knee, showing him a book of hours.[31] The habit of possessing books might never have reached the laity if writing had not been so luxurious and so covetable. Illumination introduced the laity to script through images which could not fail to attract the eye. The children of the prosperous were introduced to the Psalter by their mothers or a priest for the purpose both of learning to read and of beginning formal prayer. To own a Psalter was therefore an act of familial as well as of public piety. Fust and Schoeffer's Psalter of 1457 and the Gutenberg Bibles made the treasures of a millennium of monastic culture available to buyers. This was the first market for printing.

Perhaps only a minority of these new lay book owners read the Psalter with full understanding, but that has been true of owners of books at any time. Moreover, understanding a book meant something different to the medieval reader than it does to us. Monastic reading, *lectio divina,* was not a utilitarian procedure. In the Rule of St. Benedict, each monk was given one book to study for a year.[32] This gave him time to digest it by metaphorically chewing over its meaning. St Anselm's *Meditation on Human Redemption* (composed in the 1090s) describes the process: "Taste the goodness of your redeemer . . . chew the honeycomb of his words, suck their flavour which is sweeter than honey, swallow their wholesome sweetness; chew by thinking, suck by understanding, swallow by loving and rejoicing." [33] The process of rumination was assisted by the brilliant colors of the illuminations, "The ink with which we write is humility itself," wrote a monk of Durham in the twelfth century, while "the diverse colours wherewith the book is illuminated not unworthily represent the grace of heavenly wisdom." [34] This wisdom was the gift of the Holy Spirit, shining through fallible men. Illuminations in books had the same sort of effect as the stained glass and jewels of the great churches. They helped the worshipper through the refraction of color and light to absorb the meaning of the work into his inner being.

> Aurum nec sumptus, operis mirare laborem, Nobile claret opus, sed opus quod nobile claret clarificet mentes, ut eant per lumina vera ad verum lumen . . .
> (Marvel not at gold nor the expense but at the craftsmanship of the work. Bright is the noble work, but work which is nobly bright brightens minds, so that they go through true lights to the True Light . . .)

This verse of Abbot Suger, in praise of his gilded doors at St. Denis in 1140, applies equally well to the way illuminated books were intended to shine through to the truth.[35] Beyond *legere* (reading) was *intellegere* (understanding). Mastering the literal meaning of a text was merely the first step before proceeding to its higher meanings: allegorical (intimating eternal truths); tropological (prescribing moral duties); anagogical (anticipating future happenings).[36] Only then did the scripture make full sense. St. Paul's words "the letter killeth, but the spirit giveth life" were the basis of the medieval approach to scripture and hence to other forms of reading.[37] Perhaps this is why the earliest printing was made to look like an illuminated manuscript, "written" (in St. Paul's words) "not with ink, but with the spirit of the living God; not in tables of stone, but in fleshy tables of the heart," [38] whereas the truth was that the bed of metal type from which a printed text was produced was as insensible as a "table of stone."

Looking Back at the Other Forms of Literacy

Although works of "Sacred Literacy" stand in pride of place in the earliest printing, other pieces were produced which I have categorized as providing for "Learned Literacy," "Bureaucratic Literacy," and "Vernacular Literacy." These forms do not require as full an exposition, as they are more familiar to the modern reader. Nevertheless here also medieval forms differed from ours and contributed to the growth of literacy in surprising ways. To consider "Learned Literacy" first of all: As we have seen, this was represented in the earliest printing most frequently by Donatus, the Latin grammar which had been in continuous use for more than a millennium. Medieval attitudes to classical Latin were ambivalent. No less an authority than Pope Gregory the Great (590–604) despised grammar because he thought it "entirely unworthy to confine the words of celestial revelation within the rules of Donatus." [39] But it was an inescapable fact that the words of the scripture were confined within these rules because Aelius Donatus, the author of the grammar, taught St. Jerome, who produced the Latin vulgate Bible. Latin style was first absorbed by reading the Bible, starting in early childhood with the Psalter, and then developed formally through grammar and the study of classical authors, particularly Virgil, Cicero, and Ovid. Through teaching and copying texts, the monasteries became not only the guardians but the promoters of pagan classical learning. The school and library of Monte Cassino, the mother house of Benedictine monasticism, best demonstrate this continuity of the classical tradition in the early Middle Ages. [40]

There was of course some decline between the sixth century and the twelfth in both the quality and the quantity of Latin writing. Nevertheless this had the paradoxical effect of giving literates peculiar prestige. *Litteratus* in medieval usage meant to be learned in Latin rather than to have a rudimentary ability to read and write. [41] But Latin learning was also directly associated with the church. As a consequence the elite of the church, the *clerici,* became identified with the learned elite, the *litterati.* By the twelfth century the terms *clericus* and *litteratus* were synonymous. [42] The *clerici* had important privileges which the *litterati* consequently shared. In later medieval England the most conspicuous of such privileges was benefit of clergy whereby a person found guilty of a serious crime was exempted from the death penalty if he could prove that he was *Litteratus.* [43] The test usually consisted of reading a passage from the Psalter, which (as we have seen) was the starting point of both biblical and Latin study and was also—most appropriately—the first book to bear a printer's name and date. At the very time that printing was invented in Germany, English records demonstrate that prisoners of "every variety of occupation" including laborers were proving their "clergy" by a reading test.[44] Such a test was obviously a diminution of the earlier ideal of a *litteratus* being a person of eminent learning and status. Thus, for example, English records show that of a sample of 116 male witnesses in London between 1467 and 1476, 62 (that is, more than half) are described as *litteratus* and 6 as *aliqualiter litteratus* ("quite literate").[45] These *litterati* are primarily tradesmen and superior artisans: fishmongers, grocers, haberdashers, barbers, tailors, joiners, and so on. *Litteratus* in this context evidently has something like its modern meaning of "competent in the rudiments" rather than "learned" in the old tradition, just as *clericus* in the late Middle Ages began to mean "clerk" rather than one of the elite.

It is not my purpose here to estimate from such statistics what proportion of the population of England or of other regions of Europe was literate (in whatever sense) at the time printing was invented, although that should be done. At present I wish only to emphasize in a general way how clerical privilege promoted the growth of literacy among the laity. Probably more important than the negative aspect of avoiding the death penalty were the positive privileges of the clergy, particularly their endowments, which comprised by the fifteenth century one quarter to one third of all wealth. Clergy were needed at every level of society, from princely bishops and abbots down to poor priests in the villages. As the clergy were supposed to be celibate, new members had constantly to be recruited from the laity, and as they were supposed to be learned, some knowledge of Latin was the criterion for entry. In these ways some Latin, and hence some literacy in the medieval sense, made its way across and down the social classes. Educationists are now becoming aware that people need strong inducements to be literate. Medieval society offered its *litterati* greater privileges perhaps than any previous civilization. Certainly only medieval society made the ability to read a matter of life and death.

Another of the earliest uses of printing was for what I call "Bureaucratic Literacy," in the first instance for papal indulgence certificates. Bureaucracy was as powerful a promoter of literacy and respect for writing as either "Sacred Literacy" or "Learned Literacy." It has begun to increase markedly in the twelfth century, when secular governments followed the lead of the popes in developing chanceries and employing clerks on a regular basis.[46]

Kings began to pester their subjects with written demands, particularly for taxes, until writing penetrated into the villages. "Thou art writen y my writ that thou wel wost" (You are written in my list as you know very well), the English *Song of the Husbandman* (dating from the first decades of the fourteenth century) has the village beadle say to a peasant.[47] Unlike the other forms of literacy moreover, the growth of bureaucracy encouraged writing as much as reading, because numerous clerks were needed to write the letters and reply to them. The medieval universities grew out of this need for clerks. The earliest ones (Bologna, Paris, and Salerno) were distinguished from the monastic schools by providing a practical education in law, theology, and medicine. University masters claimed that these new subjects were superior to the classical curriculum of the Seven Liberal Arts and out of this grew the controversy of the *moderni* (the university masters and bureaucrats) and the *antiqui* (the monks and grammarians). The idea of being "modern" is itself medieval. The best example of a "modern" curriculum is the *ars dictaminis,* the art of dictation or letter writing, which was taught in law schools. The graduates of these courses became the notaries and secretaries who were indispensable to bureaucratic administration.[48]

"Sacred Literacy" gave books peculiar prestige. "Learned Literacy" made literates into a privileged elite. "Bureaucratic Literacy" caused the diffusion of documents and of their writers throughout the towns and villages of medieval Europe. Compared with all this, "Vernacular Literacy" was still making its way. Although by Gutenberg's time vernacular literature had taken shape and, in most countries had two or three centuries of growth behind it, vernacular writings do not have a large place in the earliest printing. To this rule there are local exceptions, of which Caxton's printing of Chaucer's *Canterbury Tales* is the most prominent.

The Growth of Literacy

The four forms of literacy which I have identified in the earliest printing are a useful way of looking at the development of literacy, but they have the shortcoming of all historical generalizations of being oversimplified. There was no linear growth of literacy from "Sacred" to "Learned" to "Bureaucratic" and thence to "Vernacular." The four forms were in theory mutually opposed and might have cancelled each other out. Sacred writing should not have been used for secular purposes and its painstaking script (book hand) and illuminations were unsuitable for ordinary business. Many of the early charters written by monks are absurdly unprofessional documents, both in content and appearance, by later medieval notarial standards. Learning likewise was theoretically opposed to "Sacred Literacy," as it was associated with paganism. Monastic attitudes towards it were as ambivalent in the time of St. Bernard in the twelfth century as they had been in the time of Gregory the Great. Furthermore, although the division between *clerici* and *laici* did in fact cause an increasing proportion of the population to be initiated into the clerical way of literacy, that had not been the original intention. Laymen were in theory excluded from literacy because it was in Latin. Even if a knight learned to read Latin, it did not extend his own form of culture and education because that was in the oral tradition of a vernacular language. In the words of a thirteenth-century English knight, Walter of Bibbesworth, "le levere nous aprent clergie" (the book teaches us the way of the clergy).[49] Nor was "Bureaucratic Literacy" a simple or effortless development. Documents were distrusted for the good reason that many of them (particularly monastic charters) were forgeries and they did not at first contain information to verify them, such as the date and place of issue or the writer's name. It was a legal commonplace that oral witness deserved more credence than written evidence: "Witnesses were alive and credible because they could defend their statements; writing was dead marks on a dead surface, unable to clarify itself if it proved unclear or to defend itself against objections."[50]

Instead of asking in an impatient modern way "Why did literacy not develop faster in the Middle Ages?" we should be asking "Why did it develop at all, considering the obstacles in its path?" In reply to the latter question I would suggest that although the various forms of medieval literacy pointed in different directions, they overlapped because practice was less self-contained than theory. Monks were often acquainted with pagan literature and the language of medieval scripture was unavoidably the language of Donatus. Monks too came to terms with bureaucracy and secular government. They recorded the charters of kings in their cartularies and their worldly deeds in their chronicles. Harder to understand is why monks and clerics wrote down vernacular epics like *Beowulf* and the *Chanson de Roland,* but these two had a Christian message. Similarly the schoolmen, who specialized in "Learned Literacy," had close associations with both the "Sacred" and the "Bureaucratic" forms. The purpose of the new higher learning, most obviously in theology and canon law, was to expound the authority of the Bible and the church. At the

19

same time this was a practical endeavour, brought down to the level of daily business by the *ars dictaminis* and the basic method of canon law which depended upon the interpretation of decretal letters. The most exalted of the schoolmen became saints of the church, while the majority became clerks in chanceries and the wandering scholars of the taverns. These humble literates disseminated their skills and made them attractive. From the storytellers and minstrels, grounded in the schools, came the great vernacular writers: Chretien de Troyes, Gottfried von Strasburg, Boccaccio, Chaucer. The greatest of them all, Dante, was steeped in the learning of the schools.

Thus in numerous ways the various forms of literacy reinforced each other, despite being mutually opposed in theory. As a consequence almost all medieval writings took on some of the dignity and awe of sacred books. The most secular of documents, William the Conqueror's Domesday Book, looks not unlike a prayer book (indeed later copies of it were elaborately illuminated) and, as its name *Domesdei* (Doomsday) implies, it was likened by the conquered English to the Book of Revelation and the last judgment.[51] Similarly the schoolmen, the *clerici* and *litterati*, retained their privileges despite becoming more numerous, and they glossed the books of secular roman law in the same way as they glossed the Bible. Writs and charters too were portentous documents, which adopted their conventions of style and script from sacred and scholastic works. They needed to be portentous if they were to impress the semi-literate. For example, the indulgence certificates printed by Gutenberg's press had to look like assurances of salvation and not simple receipts. Printing thus emerged not from a vacuum,· but from a rich and complex culture which gave extraordinary prestige to the written word. In the earliest printed works, Gutenberg and his associates, out of commercial necessity, identified the chief features of medieval literate culture and aimed to reproduce them as exactly as possible. In doing so, they acknowledged the achievements of a millennium of writing.

Notes

1. *L'Apparition du Livre* (Paris, 1950), trans. D. Gerard (London, 1976). Stillwell, *The Beginning of the World of Books* (New York, 1972).

2. C. M. Cipolla, *Literacy and Development in the West* (London, 1969), p. 50, citing A. F. Villemain.

3. John of Salisbury, *Metalogicon,* book 3, ch. 4, ed. C. C. J. Webb (Oxford, 1929), p. 136. A. G. Molland, "Medieval Ideas of Scientific Progress," *Journal of the History of Ideas* 39 (1978): 564–66.

4. *The Gutenberg Galaxy* (London, 1962), p. 142.

5. Ibid., pp. 142, 207. Febvre and Martin, trans. Gerard, p. 249.

6. My viewpoint as a medievalist differs from that of E. L. Eisenstein, *The Printing Press as an Agent of Change* (Cambridge, England, 1979), 2 vols.

7. The best introduction to Gutenberg is V. Scholderer, *Johann Gutenberg* (British Museum Publications, 1963). H. Lehmann-Haupt, *Gutenberg and the Master of the Playing Cards* (New Haven, 1966), pp. 47ff., argues that Gutenberg was a perfectionist. On the other hand, G. D. Painter in *Essays in Honor of V. Scholderer*, ed. D. E. Rhodes (Mainz, 1970), pp. 307–8, argues that Gutenberg had been making money on the side.

8. E. Soltész, *Biblia Pauperum: the Estergom Blockbook of Forty Leaves* (Budapest, 1967), is a useful introduction with facsimiles.

9. Lehmann-Haupt, *Gutenberg*, frontispiece and p. 3, note 1.

10. *De Laude Scriptorum*, ed. K. Arnold, trans. R. Behrendt (Kansas, 1974), ch. 7, p. 63.

11. Eisenstein, *The Printing Press*, vol. 1, pp. 14–15, 94–97.

12. *The Letters of Peter the Venerable*, ed. G. Constable (Cambridge, Mass., 1967), vol. 1, p. 38. E. R. Curtius, *European Literature and the Latin Middle Ages*, trans. W. R. Trask (London, 1953), pp. 313–14.

13. Stillwell, *The Beginning*, nos. 1, 6, 7, 12, 17, 18, 19, 21, 22, 25, 27.

14. Ibid. nos. 3, 4, 23a, 23b, 23c, 23d, 33b.

15. Ibid., nos. 13, 26, 28, 30, 35.

16. Ibid., nos. 8, 9, 10, 11, 14, 15, 20, 31, 32, 33a, 34.

17. Scholderer, *Gutenberg*, plate viii.

18. N. F. Blake, *Caxton: England's First Publisher* (London, 1976), pp. 33 (facsimile), 200.

19. Stillwell, *The Beginning*, nos. 2 (Sibyllenbuch), 29 (Ackermann von Böhmen), 5, 16, 24.

20. H. Grundmann, *"Litteratus-Illitteratus,"* *Archiv für Kulturgeschichte*, 40 (1958): 1–65.

21. R. Hirsch, "Scribal Tradition and Innovation in Early Printed Books," *The Printed Word: Its Impact and Diffusion* (London, 1978), no. xv, with facsimiles.

22. See note 7 above.

23. A reconstructed technique for doing this is illustrated by Lehmann-Haupt, *Gutenberg*, pp. 50–51.

24. Throughout this paragraph I follow T. C. Skeat, "Early Christian Book Production: Papyri and Manuscripts" in *The Cambridge History of the Bible*, ed. G. W. H. Lampe, vol. 2 (Cambridge, England, 1969), pp. 54–79. I do not have first-hand knowledge of this subject myself.

25. J. J. G. Alexander, *The Decorated Letter* (London, 1978). The best overall survey of medieval writing techniques is still W. Wattenbach, *Das Schriftwesen im Mittelalter* 4th edition (Leipzig, 1896).

26. K. Weitzmann, *Late Antique and Early Christian Book Illumination* (London, 1977).

27. The idea of the *sacra pagina* is exemplified in the citation from Peter the Venerable (note 12 above). In general, see J. Leclercq, *The Love of Learning and the Desire for God*, trans. C. Misrahi (New York, 1961), ch. 5.

28. J. J. G. Alexander, *Insular Manuscripts* (London, 1978), p. 29, no. 4.

29. M. B. Parkes, "The Literacy of the Laity," *The Medieval World*, ed. D. Daiches and A. Thorlby (London, 1973), pp. 567–68, gives English examples of bequests of books by knights and burgesses of the fourteenth and fifteenth centuries. From the thirteenth century a market developed for pocket-sized Bibles, D. Diringer, *The Illuminat-*

ed Book 2nd edition (London, 1967), p. 267.

30. For example M. J. Friedländer, *Early Netherlandish Painting*, vol. 2, *Roger van der Weyden and the Master of Flémalle* (Leyden, 1967), plates 16, 17, 59, 69, 72, 75, 78, 80. Compare other scenes of women with books, plates 2, 20, 84, 85, 97.

31. *Early Netherlandish Painting*, vol. 2, plate 137; vol. 3, plate 96; vol. 4, plates 77, 79, 80, 91; vol. 7, plate 22.

32. Rule of St. Benedict, ch 48. M. T. Clanchy, *From Memory to Written Record: England 1066-1307* (Cambridge, Mass., 1979), p. 130.

33. *Sancti Anselmi Opera Omnia*, ed. F. S. Schmitt (Seckau and Edinburgh, 1938-61), vol. 3, p. 84. Leclercq, *The Love of Learning*, p. 90. Clanchy, *From Memory*, pp. 216-17.

34. R. A. B. Mynors, *Durham Cathedral Manuscripts* (Oxford, 1939), p. 9. Curtius, *European Literature*, pp. 315-19, gives other examples of this genre of metaphor.

35. E. Panofsky, *Abbot Suger on the Abbey Church of St. Denis* (Princeton, 1946), pp. 46-48, and comment at pp. 19-24, 164-65. On scribal technique being concerned with "light *through, not* light *on*" see McLuhan, *The Gutenberg Galaxy*, pp. 105-6 and the works there cited.

36. J. Pelikan, *The Growth of Medieval Theology* (Chicago, 1978), p. 40.

37. 2 Corinthians 3:6. In general, see B. Smalley, *The Study of the Bible in the Middle Ages* 2nd edition (Oxford, 1952), ch. 1.

38. 2 Corinthians 3:3.

39. Prologue to "Moralia in Job," *Sancti Gregorii Papae I Opera Omina*, vol. 1, Patrologiae Latinae, vol. 75, column 516. Leclercq, *The Love of Learning*, p. 60.

40. H. Block, "Monte Cassino's Teachers and Library in the High Middle Ages" in *La Scuola nell'Occidente Latino dell'Alto Medioevo*, Centro Italiano di Studi sull'Alto Medioevo (Spoleto, 1972), vol. 2, pp. 563-602. In general, see P. Riché, *Education and Culture in the Barbarian West* (Columbia, 1976) and *Les Ecoles et l'Enseignement dans l'Occident Chrétion de la Fin du Ve Siècle au Milieu du Xle Siècle* (Paris, 1979).

41. See note 20 above.

42. Clanchy, *From Memory*, p. 178.

43. J. H. Baker, *The Reports of Sir John Spelman*, vol. 2, Selden Society 94 (London, 1978), pp. 327-34 of the Introduction.

44. L. C. Gabel, *Benefit of Clergy in the Later Middle Ages*, Smith College Studies in History 14 (1929), p. 81.

45. Ibid., pp. 82-84. N. Orme, *English Schools in the Middle Ages* (London, 1973), p. 50.

46. Clanchy, *From Memory*, graph at p. 44.

47. Ibid., p. 31.

48. M. T. Clanchy, "*Moderni* in Education and Government in England," *Speculum* 50 (1975): 685-86.

49. *Le Traité de Walter de Bibbesworth sur la Langue Française*, ed. A. Owen (Paris, 1929), p. 51. Clanchy, *From Memory*, p. 151.

50. W. J. Ong, reviewing Clanchy, *From Memory* in *Manuscripta* 23 (1979): 179.

51. Clanchy, *From Memory*, p. 18.

The Environment for Literacy: Accomplishment and Context in Seventeenth-Century England and New England

by David Cressy

David Cressy, a historian at Claremont Graduate School, has been working in the area of literacy studies since his undergraduate years at the University of Cambridge. He is the author of Literacy and the Social Order: Reading and Writing In Tudor and Stuart England *(Cambridge, Eng.: Cambridge University Press, 1980) and other books and articles.*

For the past few years, he has been doing work on England and America in the seventeenth and eighteenth centuries. In the paper that follows, he looks at the cultural context for literacy in the two societies and why it spread. He is particularly concerned with the economic determinants of literacy growth.

High claims were made for literacy by a succession of writers from the sixteenth century onward. In England and in New England, among churchmen and businessmen, there was a widespread belief that reading and writing were essential skills which led to a broad range of benefits. Most writers stressed the spiritual and religious advantages in being able to grapple directly with the word of God in the Bible, and some of them drew attention to the worldly advantages associated with being able to write. And most of them, whether explicitly or implicitly, associated literacy with a variety of civic and moral benefits, as if it were the indispensable correlate of civilization.

Reforming bishops in Elizabethan England urged "every man to read the Bible in Latin or English, as the very word of God and the spiritual food of man's soul, whereby they may better know their duties to God, to their sovereign lord the king, and their neighbour." This was a theme that was frequently echoed in Puritan writing of the seventeenth century. George Swinnock in *The Christian Man's Calling* lamented, "alas, the people perish for want of knowledge. And how can they know God's will that cannot read it?" The English Puritan Richard Baxter in *A Christian Directory* admonished parents, "by all means let children be taught to read, if you are never so poor and whatever shift you make, or else you deprive them of a singular help to their instruction and salvation." Instruction and salvation were the two benefits of literacy which were repeatedly proclaimed throughout the seventeenth century, with frequent references to the "mercy" or "profit" attached to the skill. Baxter, for example, claimed that "it is a very great mercy to be able to read the holy scriptures for themselves, and a very great misery to know nothing but what they hear from others." This last remark touches on one of the crucial disadvantages that was generally associated with illiteracy; without the ability to read you would not only remain ignorant, but you would constantly be dependent on others. Without literacy you were not only cut off from direct knowledge of the holy text, but worse, you would fall short in your duty and be much more open to error.[1]

Nor were these the only sad consequences of illiteracy. A catalog of evils was invoked to warn of the dangers of inadequate education. Without literacy to guide them in godliness, it was feared that children might become "idle . . . vile and abject persons, liars, thieves, evil beasts, slow bellies and good for nothing." The inability to read and to write, the absence of a discriminating education through paper and print, could usher in "rudeness, licentiousness, profaneness, superstition, and any wickedness." Among preachers and teachers, on both sides of the Atlantic, there was a widespread fear that without literacy there would be barbarity, "a generation of barbarians in a Christian happy land." This tradition found voice in English Puritans like William Gouge and Richard Baxter, and in New England clergymen like Samuel Willard. Preaching at Boston in 1707, Willard stressed the "usefulness" of literacy and its importance for "the way of salvation." The lack of it had huge and troublesome ramifications. "The want of it [literacy] renders persons unfit for many services, which otherwise they might profit by, and through this defect they render themselves contemptible." This was bad enough and might have practical implications in the colonial community. But there was more. "When we consider that God hath stored the hidden treasures of wisdom in the records of his Word, which must lie by as a book sealed, as to those that cannot read, doubtless all parents that have regard to the souls of their

children will be very careful to obtain for them this benefit, the neglect hereof must leave them guilty of brutish inhumanity." Other examples might be found, with greater and lesser degrees of pulpit rhetoric, but the tradition they represent is clear: literacy was the key to the success and survival of a reformed Christian culture.[2]

Reading and writing could also be credited with securing a variety of secular benefits which were equally important for cultural cohesion. Literacy and education could combat "misorders" and "disobedience" and could promote "policy and civility." Plenty of authors were willing to testify to "the vast usefulness of reading" and to argue that writing was the "key . . . to the descrying and finding out of innumerable treasures." Through writing, according to David Brown, "all high matters of whatsoever nature or importance are both intended and prosecuted, secret matters are secretly kept, friends that be a thousand miles distant are conferred with and (after a sort) visited; the excellent works of godly men, the grave sentences of wise men, and the profitable arts of learned men, who died a thousand years ago, are yet extant for our daily use and imitation; all the estates, kingdoms, cities and countries of the world are governed, laws and printing maintained, justice and discipline administered, youth bred in piety, virtue, manners and learning at schools and universities, and that which is most and best, all the churches of God from the beginning established and always to this day edified." [3]

This was as noble and eloquent an argument for literacy as could be wished. Reading was a tool for cultural integration and could keep you in touch with people and ideas across the centuries and across the miles. By programming that reading as a corpus of godly texts, a curriculum of select classical learning, or a flow of political and administrative instruction, the leaders of society could embrace, and to some extent control, the literate population.

The practical, day-to-day benefits of literacy could be even more compelling. Those who were indifferent to godliness and civility might be touched by an argument which appealed to pocket and pride. Illiteracy might be socially damaging. According to David Brown, "not to write at all is both shame and scathe [hurt]." The embarrassment of illiteracy might prejudice your business dealings; the scrivener or your partner might take advantage of your defect and through illiteracy you might "lose some good design." But worse than being tricked by someone with superior technical capability was the insult to one's self-esteem and public reputation. "It is shame both to employ a

notar to subscribe for thee in any security, and to want that good token of education which perhaps thine inferior hath, for wheresoever any man of honest rank resorteth who cannot write, chiefly where he is not known, he is incontinent esteemed either to be base born or to have been basely brought up in a base or moorland desert, that is, far from any city where there be schools of learning, discipline, policy and civility." [4]

This theme was recurrent in the writings of professional educators. Martin Billingsley insisted that writing provided a defense against "the manifold deceits of this world" and stressed its particularly utility for the protection of widows. A century later Thomas Dilworth rehearsed a similar argument, claiming "that both sexes should be alike ready at their pen. . . . How often do we see women when they are left to shift for themselves in the melancholy state of widowhood (and what woman knows that she shall not be left in the like state?) obliged to leave their business to the management of others; sometimes to their great loss, and sometimes to their utter ruin; when at the contrary had they been ready at their pen, could spell well and understand figures, they might not only have saved themselves from ruin, but perhaps have been mistresses of good fortunes." [5]

We should be careful when reading these advertisements by professional teachers, just as we should be careful when reading the urgings of religious reformers, to separate the attitudes and motivations of the authors from the reality of the world they describe. David Brown, for example, was himself newly arrived in London from Scotland and knew how to work on the insecurities of his customers. Writing masters could fan and enlarge fears about the pitfalls of illiteracy, and might even plant them, to stimulate the market. In a similar vein, the preachers, like Samuel Willard with his remark about the contempt which might befall the illiterate, were creating an image and firming a commitment rather than describing a situation. We really do not know whether ordinary people in everyday circumstances felt shamed by the limitations of their literacy or experienced frustration or complication in their designs. In both its religious and its secular strands, the rhetorical stream was insistent on the value of literacy, but that does not prove that the population at large agreed with its sentiments or experienced the problems or delights to which it referred. Before agreeing with the proponents of literacy and endorsing their remarks, remarks which in many cases sound similar to those made by modern educators or custodians of cultural policy, we should evaluate the context in which they were

uttered and the world to which they belonged. Literacy may turn out to have been less crucial than might be imagined.

The importance of literacy varied with circumstances. In one social situation, in one place or time, the ability to read and write was of unquestionable importance. The affairs of some people might be of such a complexity, their aspirations of such a richness, that literacy was essential. Other people in simpler circumstances might have no such need of those skills. The literacy needs of neighboring communities could be entirely different, especially if one was enmeshed in the market economy while the other was mainly bucolic. Different individuals made different uses of literacy in their lives, depending on their social position or occupation, their family arrangements, and their religous persuasion. This relativity is borne out by both qualitative and quantitative evidence from England, New England, and other early modern societies. It is important to talk of the margins of literacy, gradations of literacy, and of the uneven incidence of literacy in a partially literate society, rather than the simple dichotomy of literacy and illiteracy.

In England in the seventeenth century, as in centuries before, a competent and contented life could be lived without the intrusion of literate skills. The countryman, according to Nicholas Breton, could perform his seasonal tasks from year to year without recourse to reading and writing. "We can learn to plough and harrow, sow and reap, plant and prune, thresh and fan, winnow and grind, brew and bake, and all without book. These are our chief business in the country, except we be jurymen to hang a thief or speak truth in a man's right which conscience and experience will teach us with a little learning." [6] Why should the husbandman send his son to school, at cost of time and money, if the skills he would then bring home had no obvious immediate application? Who needed to be able to read and write if he had standing enough with his neighbors already, was possessed of an adequate mind and memory, and had learned and could pass on his knowledge of animals, the land and the weather through observation and practice? He might even grow prosperous and go to heaven without being able to sign his name, since neither wealth nor salvation were hinged exclusively to literacy.

This last point, which cuts against the grain of early modern discussions of literacy, requires amplification. Traditionalists had never conceded that Bible literacy was essential in religious devotion, and Thomas More had observed during the stormy first decade of the Reformation, "many . . . shall with God's grace,

though they never read a word of scripture, come as well to heaven." Despite the evangelical insistence on reading, the church in England continued to stress the oral elements of liturgical worship and catechetical instruction. Psalms could be sung and sermons could be heard without the complications of print. The Protestant revolution notwithstanding, it was not necessary to be literate to be devout, and entry into the Kingdom of Heaven was not conditional on being able to read. Richard Steele, in a set of sermons entitled *The Husbandmans Calling,* told his country congregation, "though you cannot read a letter in the book, yet you can by true assurance read your name in the Book of Life, your scholarship will serve. . . . if you cannot write a word, yet see you transcribe a fair copy of a godly righteous and sober life, and you have done well." [7]

In his other roles too the husbandman was under no pressure to become literate. As tenant and farmer, subject and householder, the world of print and script made few inroads into his life. Whether he dealt with the manor court, quarter sessions, or church courts, all courts of record with a high turnover of paper and ink, his participation was oral, interlocutory, and required no mastery of reading and writing. The church courts, for example, made sure that "the registrar or examiner have a great care in explaining and declaring distinctly and plainly to witnesses all and singular the heads and contents of these articles and positions." If he had to set his name to a document it was first read out to him, and it made no difference if he signed with a mark instead of a signature. An illiterate's mark had equal weight in law to the most flourishing autograph signature, and there seems to have been no shame or hesitation in signing with a cross. [8]

With such small incentive to acquire literacy, and little enough to do with it if you had it, it is not surprising to discover that most husbandmen stood apart from the world of reading and writing. Four out of five of them could not sign their own names. A study of four English regions between 1560 and 1730 finds 73 percent to 91 percent of the husbandmen made marks instead of signatures on depositions, a level that was only worsted by laborers and some of the roughest outdoor trades like thatchers and miners, for whom the utility of literacy was similarly underdeveloped. In East Anglia, a prosperous area which sent a significant number of emigrants to colonial America, 79 percent of the husbandmen were unable to sign, and the proportion grew higher rather than lower as the seventeenth century progressed. Despite the urgings of reformers, despite the presence in the region of a large number of schoolteachers, and despite all the

blandishments of puritanism and the "educational revolution," a huge proportion of the agrarian population remained indifferent to literacy.[9]

The benefits of literacy were circumstantial. As one moved from the level of husbandman to yeoman, from copyholder to freeholder, from subsistence farming to production for the market, the ability to read and to write grew appreciably in importance. As the complexity of one's dealings increased, so did the advantage of being able to decipher writing and record things on paper. The farmer who could jot down market prices and compare them from week to week or season to season could secure a commercial advantage over his illiterate neighbor, who relied on his memory. Financial transactions would grow in volume and complexity to the point that David Brown's remarks about the "scathe" of illiteracy become meaningful. The yeoman who could write bonds and receipts for himself and otherwise dispose of his affairs in writing would develop a commercial fluency and would be free of the expense and possible untrustworthiness of the scrivener or writing man. Reading and writing would become *useful* and thereby worth knowing. The yeoman's practical literacy might include the reading of handbills and almanacs and might extend to works on husbandry and self-improvement. Almanacs contained a store of usable information, weights and measures, fairs and distances, medical and culinary advice, as well as calendrical information, and might be referred to more frequently than the Bible. Certainly the circulation of almanacs was large enough by the end of the seventeenth century for a copy to have been on most yeomen's shelves.

The quantitative evidence shows that literacy was indeed more developed among yeomen. In the seventeenth century, no more than a third of them were unable to sign their names, and there was further improvement by the end of the period. Only 24 percent of the yeomen sampled in East Anglia in the 1660s could not sign, while in the southwest at that time the figure was 20 percent.[10] Among this class of men—independent, and by all accounts prosperous, farmers—the practical advantages of literacy could be tangible and immediate. It did not take a preacher or teacher commending spiritual or ideological benefits to persuade a yeoman to prize the skills of reading and writing and to secure them for his children. What little we know about attendance patterns at country schools suggests that the yeomen and the shop-keeping classes were their major patrons. Even establishments intended for "the poor" appear to have had primarily a superior freeholding and commercial clientele. The real poor were poorly

motivated, while the social and occupational groups most engaged in buying and selling, lending and leasing, kept up a
steady demand for education.

That demand was secular and practical. As Nicholas Breton's
yeoman explains: "This is all we go to school for: to read
common prayers at church and set down common prices at
market, write a letter and make a bond, set down the day of our
births, our marriage day, and make our wills when we are sick for
the disposing of our goods when we are dead. These are the
chief matters that we meddle with and we find enough to trouble
our heads withal." [11] This may be too narrow a depiction because there were Bible-reading activists among the yeoman, and
some of them bought books for entertainment as well as for practical purposes. But that too may have been environmentally appropriate. The yeoman was popularly regarded as being on the
heels of the gentleman, aping his letters and picking up scraps of
his culture. A taste for literature, or at least a display of books,
may have been one more way of impressing one's status on the
community.

In the nonagrarian sector of the economy, even more than
on the land, there was a graduated or differential value attached
to literacy. Varying degrees of familiarity and competence were
required, or were at least suited, for different types of occupation. Among townsmen of various sorts and among tradesmen
and craftsmen in the country, the level of skill in reading and
writing might vary with the frequency and complexity of their
dealings on paper. To achieve or sustain a position among the
mercantile elite, full fluency with print and script was virtually indispensable. Active literacy went with business acumen in pursuing commercial opportunities, keeping abreast of trade regulations and shipping news, preparing financial records, and corresponding with associates. Along the wharves and counting houses
of London and Boston, literacy might almost be taken for granted, although it was still possible to smell a profit without a literate education. Literacy was also useful to shopkeepers and specialist craftsmen, people like haberdashers and goldsmiths, and it
could be an asset to retailers and commercial artisans lower
down the social scale. But manual workers and village craftsmen,
carpenters and bricklayers, might find no more use for reading
and writing than did the majority of husbandmen.

It was conventional in the seventeenth century to distinguish
between those engaged in "marchandize" and those engaged in
"manuarie," separating the merchants and tradesmen from the
artisans and "mechanicks." This was a division for the purposes

of social analysis which recognized different cultural realms as well as different economic activities. It is also suggestive of a cleavage in the utility, practical significance, and integration of literacy.[12]

One of the clearest acknowledgements of the importance of literacy is found in the extensive last will and testament of Robert Keayne, a Boston merchant of the seventeenth century. Keayne used his will, a fifty-thousand word rambling apologia, to demonstrate to his friends, enemies, associates, and posterity that his business affairs were consonant with the standards of the community. To assist his heirs and executors, and to vindicate his troubled reputation, Keayne drew attention to his various manuscript notebooks.[13]

"Almost everything which belongs to my estate is by myself committed to writing in one book or other, either in my day book of what I buy or sell, or in my debt book of which there is chiefly three in use, namely, one bound in brown vellum which I call my vellum debt book, the other bound in thin parchment which I call the new debt book, the third is bound in white vellum, which I keep constantly in my closet at Boston and is called my book of creditors and debtors. . . . There is also in my closet a long white paper book bound in white parchment which I call my inventory book, in which I do yearly, commonly, cast up my whole estate." Keayne evidently regarded his records as more than a mere financial archive, although that by itself was a potent use of the pen. More important, they were testimony to his transactions, a history of his dealings and relationships, and they could be called upon to settle agruments in years to come. Old writings could have current value, in exactly the manner envisaged by David Brown.

Applied literacy gave a documentary firmness to transactions which could be disputed if they simply turned on a handshake or verbal agreement. Literacy offered proof. Keayne's set of papers, "some of which though they be evened and quite discharged long ago and crossed, yet I keep them by me, that if any wrangling person pretending ignorance should call things to an account again, as some have done, by having recourse to these books and papers I can show them when and how and in what it was discharged and evened. Therefore very few of those papers are to be neglected or cast by, as if they were kept for no use at all."

Keayne even kept records by him in New England which documented his dealings and obligations from the years before he emigrated from old England. This archival retentiveness may have saved his career. Challenged about an old English £200 debt, long since discharged, Keayne turned to his documents. "I looked in all my papers and writings where I thought it might be, but could find none, for in such a remove many writings might be lost, or at least so mixed up with other things so long out of date, that there might be no hope of finding it." Keayne's reputation suffered through this dislocation of his filing system, but eventually, "after long search amongst many books and papers I found the receipt of it in this book, being before utterly denied that it was ever paid." Such a vindication was only possible through active writing and with preservation of the written record. Here was the utility of literacy demonstrated with a vengeance.

Robert Keayne was one of the richest men in the colonies and had business and social dealings of various sorts throughout the Atlantic world. At his level it was quite natural that reading and writing should play a major role in his affairs. The surviving account books, letter books, and business journals demonstrate a similar mastery of practical literacy among other international tradesmen of his time. Keayne also went in for authorship on religious and military subjects, and in this too he was not unique. But lower down the commercial scale, among those more common beings who bought and sold in less profusion and who had less active dealings in land, full and confident literacy was a less urgent matter.

Someone could always be found to set your affairs in the appropriate written form. No doubt it was more satisfactory to be able to read and write if you were buying land, disposing of goods, engaging in trade, or trying to keep in touch with a distant relative, but one was not entirely incapacitated by illiteracy. A scrivener, secretary, or free-lance writing man could accomplish the task, and if the occasions were not too frequent and the service not too costly, there was no pressing need to acquire literacy for oneself. Writings by proxy had as much force in law, and the fact of illiteracy was no necessary hindrance to a career. William Shakespeare's father never learned to write, but he could still fulfill his duties as an alderman of Stratford.[14] Hundreds of local officials in the seventeenth century made marks instead of signatures, while illiterate farmers and craftsmen got on with their business with no apparent sense of deprivation. A mark would serve as an authentication, and a writing man could draw up the rest of the document.

Glimpses of this activity are found on both sides of the Atlantic in the notebooks of men who served as occasional informal secretaries. Roger Lowe, a shopkeeper in provincial England, recorded some of the times he wrote letters, composed wills or cast accounts for people in his vicinity, sharing his literacy with his illiterate neighbors. In 1663, for example, "John Hasleden . . . told me that he loved a wench in Ireland, and so the day after I writ a love letter for him into Ireland." Most of his writing services were of a much more mundane nature. In New England about the same time, John Barton, a physician at Marblehead, performed the same sort of service for his unlettered neighbors. In 1673, for example, he earned 2 shillings "for writing a lease" and 1s.6d. for writing a petition. Other entries in his account book refer to miscellaneous writings, including 2s. earned from William Lake in 1674 "for making 3 bills of lading, a letter, a compt to the court." Physicians, shopkeepers, schoolmasters, clergymen, indeed, anyone in the community who was known to be adept with his pen, all could be pressed into occasional service on behalf of the less well-educated. Scribal services were widely available.[15]

There is a tendency among cultural, social, and intellectual historians to applaud the champions and promoters of literacy in the past and to commiserate with the benighted masses who lacked that package of skills. Literacy is associated with progress, with rationality, with modernity, with competence, and a host of similar abstractions of which we are supposed to approve. The pitfalls of illiteracy, sketched with such passion by the puritan preachers, are readily accepted as real disabilities, because all of us know that literacy is indispensable today. Such sentiments may be fined for a modernist, but they do not help the historian. If we return to the environment of the preindustrial world, a pluralistic environment in which literacy and illiteracy coexisted, we may find that people, for the most part, were comfortable with or without literate skills.

The oral world, with its traditions and tales, proverbs and jokes, customs and ceremonies, provided a store of enrichment and entertainment which required no literacy for access. Face-to-face communication, the sharing of stories and songs, the retelling of news and gossip, offered information and diversion enough. This culture of speech and action gave the illiterate person his bearings, but it was not at all closed to one who could read and write. Nor was the culture of print and script debarred from the illiterate. The two worlds interacted, mingled, merged. It would be wrong to think of a strict dichotomy. In practice there was feedback and linkage, and all sorts of bridging both ways.[16] Information and stimulation of a visual, oral, and traditional kind continued to be used by masters of literacy, while thoughts and expressions which at one time appeared in print could easily spill over into conversation. Folksingers, for example, could broaden their repertoire from printed broadsides, while ballad printers might collect their material from illiterate performers. Only one reader was necessary in any assembly at alehouse or market for a printed item to be decoded and made publicly available. The nonreaders might miss the nuances, and might indeed get the whole thing wrong, but bridging of this kind could also achieve the most widespread disseminating of news.

Another glimpse of the spreading of news in the period before newspapers and of the admixture of oral and literate elements in communication is provided by the work of the authorized town criers. English market towns had their criers and so did seventeenth-century Boston. Notices of importance were "cried" at the meeting house, where presumably those in attendance could read, and then "cried" around the town from street to street, where there were probably some who could not. In addition to these public duties, the Boston town criers were "to cry lost and found goods" and "to keep a book of what they cry." The town crier was a walking, shouting bulletin board. From a text delivered to him in writing he had to cry out public messages, while the classified advertisements, which may have come to him by word of mouth, were to be set down in his book of record. Literacy was a prerequisite of the job, along with a lusty voice, although the social standing that went with it is suggested by the additional duties assigned to the crier in 1666, "to clear the streets of carrion and other offensive matters." [17]

Much of the cultural life of the seventeenth century was not strictly oral or literate, but a combination of both. Important documents were read out loud as well as filed for the record. Proclamations were proclaimed as well as posted. Personal letters might be read out loud to a circle of friends, as well as read privately at home. Occasions like these served to open the literate world to the uneducated and gave an extra dimension of voice and ceremony to those who needed such assistance.

The sermon, par excellence, was a hybrid product, involving measures of literate and nonliterate activity. In New England, and in the preaching tradition in old England, the sermon was a direct, auditory experience, live from the pulpit. "This way," said Richard Baxter, "the milk cometh warmest from the breast." [18] Like theater, with which it may have more in common than is usually acknowledged, the sermon could be experienced and enjoyed by one with little or no literacy, while just a few seats away the same performance could be savored by a listener who was fully familiar with the texts under discussion and the most learned commentaries on them. In preparation for his sermon the preacher may have spent hours in his library, reading and taking notes, and an equal amount of time in quiet reflection. He may have committed his text to paper and then read it to his congregation, or he may have spoken extemporaneously from the briefest outline. Some among his listeners might be taking notes, for later study or for wider dissemination, while the sermonist himself might retrospectively revise or improve his text for publication. An oral performance, a sermon as much as a play-script, could fly with winged words and then become memorialized as a text.

The argument that literacy was primarily an environmental response gains extra strength from an examination of the actual distribution of basic literacy in early modern society. Whether we proceed geographically or in terms of social structure, it is apparent that literacy was present where it was needed and absent where it was not. At the risk of tautology, and the further risk of espousing an ecological determinism, I want to draw attention to concentrations of literacy in places where reading and writing were especially applicable, and among social groups whose need for literacy was likewise developed. There are of course exceptions and counter examples, but the central tendency is clear.

If we take a large regional or national overview in the seventeenth century, we can distinguish contrasting areas of literate development. In France, for example, the north and east were more accomplished than the south and west. The far north of England was more illiterate than the area around London, while the English settlers of Massachusetts Bay were much more fluent with reading and writing than their contemporaries in the outlying parts of New England or in the southern colonies.[19] Cultural and ideological pressures were certainly influential, but the factor which ties together these pathfinder regions for literacy was their level of economic development. Their overall environment was more demanding of literacy. This is even more clear at the local level. Farming communities were less literate than trading communities, while within the world of agriculture there were cultural, educational, and economic differences between commercial grain growers and family subsistence farms, between suppliers of meat for the urban market and upland or marshland shepherds. Margaret Spufford made this point about the contrasting communities of Cambridgeshire, and it helps us to understand the extraordinary patchwork pattern which characterised literacy at the local level.[20]

Narrowing our focus from countries to regions to counties to districts we find more variety than homogeneity. Roger Schofield observed this in eighteenth-century England, finding a greater range of literacy and illiteracy within counties than between them, and it was certainly true too in the seventeenth century. Community studies in France and America, if they penetrated below the level of the department or county to the village or township, would no doubt find similar confusion. William Gilmore has found this in the upper Connecticut Valley at the end of the eighteenth century and associates the pattern primarily with "the development of the market economy . . . the higher the level of market activity the greater the need for elementary literacy skills." [21]

The argument can be illustrated from seventeenth-century Essex. Essex, as everyone knows, was a "puritan" county adjacent to London, staunch on the parliamentary side in the civil war and generous in its supply of emigrants to New England. It is no surprise to find that Essex was among the most literate counties in England. Whereas some 70 percent of the adult male population of England was illiterate to the extent that they could not sign their names at the beginning of the civil war, the best available evidence points to a figure in Essex of 63 percent. Yet within this small county, parochial illiteracy rates ranged from 36 percent to 85 percent.[22] Attempts to explain the variation in terms of the religious complexion of each community lead only to frustration, while the most satisfactory explanation relates literacy to the claims of the environment.

Hadleigh, for example, had all the marks of a "puritan" parish. The earl of Warwick was patron of the living and installed a succession of radical ministers. Nathaniel Ward was there in the 1630s, and the parish was quick to support parliament in endorsing the Protestation, Vow and Covenant, and Solemn League and Covenant. Yet three-quarters or more of the men of Hadleigh were illiterate! When the Protestation was tendered to them, 82 percent could not sign their own names. And why should they? Hadleigh was a marshland community along the Thames estuary. Its principal economic activity was sheep grazing, and most of its householders were shepherds. Its inhabitants no doubt had full command of the mysteries of cheese and wool and animals and grass, and had little need for quill pens or books. An occupational tabulation of illiteracy in rural England places shepherds at the extremity, with 82 percent of those sampled unable to sign their names, and there is no reason to suppose that their attributes were much different in Essex.

Middleton, by contrast, was the sort of community the Puritans looked on with despair. Its cavalier clergyman, William Frost, enforced the Laudian reverence for the altar and proclaimed the antisabbatarian Book of Sports. Eventually he was ejected as an enemy to the proceedings of parliament, but even under Laud he was found guilty of drunkenness and had to purge himself of charges of incest and adultery. There was no school in the parish, and the ecclesiastical records show no presence of a freelance or licensed schoolmaster. Yet for all this, Middleton was respectably literate, with only 57 percent unable to sign. Middleton was in the prosperous grain-growing and mixed-farming region of north Essex and was only a short walk from the commercial and cloth manufacturing town of Sudbury in Suffolk. The occupational mix at Middleton included yeomen and independent craftsmen, and it was the stimulus of the economic environment rather than the influence of the pulpit which accounted for its relatively advanced literacy. In other examples, extensive literacy might be found in a community heavily exposed to puritan education, but in England, and I suspect in New England, widespread literacy rests first and firmly on economic and environmental foundations.

The social distribution of literacy in preindustrial England was more closely associated with economic activities than with anything else. A study of more than ten thousand signed or marked depositions reveals a similar profile in all parts of England from the sixteenth to the eighteenth centuries.[23] Literacy was a powerful marker of social position, and distinctive levels of accomplishment were found among different clusters of occupations. At every level literacy was a function of need, an appropriate tool for a particular range of activities.

The gentry, professional men, and merchants were virtually all in possession of literacy, and they used reading and writing in all their affairs—to get rich and stay that way, to solidify ideas and gain access to others, and to service and extend their hegemony. John Winthrop and Robert Keayne would be good examples, and at their level we should be considering the quality of literacy rather than the fact of its possession. In the next cluster, at some distance, would be found yeomen and tradesmen, who in turn maintained a solid superiority over humbler artisans, husbandmen, and laborers. This stratification is indicated in the following table.

Clusters of Illiteracy in Rural England, 1580–1700*

Percent Illiterate	Economic Activity	Social Status
0–10	merchants retailers distributors	gentry and clergy
14–33	specialist crafts	
37–52	manufacturers processors	yeomen
56–68	village crafts	
73–100	heavy manual trades	husbandmen laborers

*Based on table 68, *Literacy and the Social Order,* p. 136.

In all parts of England the ability or inability to sign followed the gradient from clean, respectable commercial pursuits, through various types of specialist craft activities, to rough, manual, outdoor occupations. The commercial elite, the merchants especially but also apothecaries, drapers, grocers, haberdashers, mercers, and similar superior shopkeepers, had a high degree of functional, practical literacy. Their routine business included correspondence, bills of sale, ledger entries, and memoranda, and their writing skills were appropriately developed. Most of the business records which survive from the seventeenth century belonged to people in this category.

The next cluster included a variety of skilled craftsmen and businessmen of the second rank, men like goldsmiths and clothiers, innkeepers and saddlers, with no more than a third of them unable to sign their names. These men were among the cream of the working population, providing specialist services and expensively wrought products. Their success depended more on experience or dexterity than a capacity for data management, but literacy would be useful for record-keeping or for keeping track of suppliers and customers. Their general ability to write their names distinguished them from the middle-ranking artisans in the third cluster and shows that they shared certain characteristics with yeomen.

The third cluster was comprised of "the industrious sort of people," between 37 percent and 52 percent illiterate. Many of them were involved in the textile industry, like woolcombers, weavers, and fullers, while others were engaged in the processing of agricultural produce, as brewers and maltsters, or in manufacturing articles of dress, as tailors and cordwainers. Very few made much use of literacy in their day-to-day employment, but some of them found reading and writing valuable as their trade expanded into a business. Literacy could be quite useful in relations with middlemen and dealers, although a surrogate or proxy could readily be found if the writing became too complex.

A fourth cluster stands out with illiteracy in the range of 56 percent to 68 percent. It included blacksmiths and carpenters, millers and butchers, who were men of simpler skills and lower esteem. These were typical of the independent craftsmen found in nearly every village. With professional skills that were mostly manual and business horizons which were mostly local there was little need for them to have received a literate education.

Finally, steeped in illiteracy was a cluster of tradesmen whose ability to write a signature was comparable to that of the husbandmen and laborers. Building workers like bricklayers, thatchers, and masons, men engaged in mineral extraction like helliers and miners, and all-weather workmen like fishermen and shepherds were rarely able to write their names. Most of their work was heavy and dirty, required more brawn than brain, and often isolated its practitioners from regular contact with the rest of society. Paper and writing rarely came their way, and if it did someone else would have to interpret it for them and be satisfied with their autograph in the form of a mark.

Preindustrial England was a partially literate society and the distribution of basic writing skills closely followed the gradient and steps of the social and economic structure. England was not unique in this regard, and similar profiles can be drawn in other societies where information about the ability to sign can be checked against status and occupation. Sixteenth-century Poland, for example, had a social distribution of literacy which was remarkably like that of Elizabethan England. In New England too the ability to sign was strongly associated with wealth and position, and a ranking can be constructed which would compare with the clusters of illiteracy in seventeenth-century England. Kenneth Lockridge, who assembled the New England evidence, prefers not to emphasize this point, stressing instead the intense drive of protestantism; but the distribution of literacy in colonial America could also be explained in terms of the economic environment.[24] The ability to read may well have been vital on Sunday, but in a world of litigation and land transfers with a high degree of involvement in local government and trade, the components of literacy could be valuable every day of the week. It was, perhaps, the combination of religion and utility, rather than protestantism alone, which singled out New England as the most literate society of all in the preindustrial world, although the region was nevertheless still stratified.

Some people in some places might be persuaded into literacy or have the ability to read and write grafted onto them in the wake of a pulpit campaign or through the philanthropic provision of education. In Sweden, for example, a persistent campaign by the state-supported Lutheran church brought most of the population across the threshold of reading and kept that skill alive through regular examination.[25] In England and New England there were educators and divines who similarly sought to promote widespread literacy, but without massive funding and legislative commitment they were unable to make much headway. However persuasive the rhetoric, it foundered on the indifference to literacy of the bulk of the population, who saw no practical need for those abilities. Where people needed little literacy to manage their affairs, and where they felt no deprivation by their educational shortcomings, it was difficult to persuade them to embrace a skill which was, for all practical purposes, superfluous.

Literacy would develop most strongly where it was relevant. This could happen even if the ideological message was ambivalent or unsupportive of popular education. In England in the seventeenth century, there was a body of opinion that was hostile to the expansion of education and which saw popular literacy as a nightmare; but this could not stop the growth of literacy among sectors of the population which decided they needed it, any more than the Puritan promoters could induce literacy in areas which were resistant. The actual profile of literacy owed nothing much to the opinions of the elite. Among some groups it was regarded as an essential skill; in others it was a desirable accomplishment; while elsewhere it was barely useful at all. Everything hinged on the demands of the environment.

In the century of Shakespeare and Bacon, Milton and Cromwell, Newton and Locke, the vast bulk of the English population was illiterate. In the eighteenth century, an age of technical invention and industrial revolution, with a far-flung empire and domestic newspapers and banking, still 50 percent or more of the population was illiterate. Throughout this period there were educational and religious leaders who espoused the views of David Brown and Richard Baxter, and there was little letup in the recommendation of literacy. Yet most of their message fell on stony ground.

If there is a lesson in all this for those trying to achieve mass literacy in the traditionally illiterate parts of the world today, or among those seeking to combat adult illiteracy in the industrialized countries, it can best be expressed in the words of a proverb: "you can lead a horse to water but you cannot make him drink." Illiteracy is not a disease, to be eradicated like yellow fever, but rather it is a complex cultural condition linked to expectations and circumstances and rooted in the environment. It may be possible, with programs, plant, and persistence, to "attack the problem" of illiteracy, but there should be no surprise if the "target population" is resistant. It may be analogous to teaching Fortran to a literature scholar. It is alien and external until a situation arises in which it can be useful. At the bridging stage there will be students and specialists to help with programming and to tend the terminal, but eventually, if the humanist's research comes to need the computational or organizational capacity of the language, he will learn it himself. Literacy will flourish where those who are offered it are aware of and can experience its benefits.

Notes

1. W. H. Frere, *Visitation Articles and Injunctions of the Period of the Reformation* (London, 1910), vol. 3, p. 301, vol. 2, p. 20. George Swinnock, *The Christian Mans Calling . . . the Second Part* (London, 1663), pp. 22–23. Richard Baxter, *A Christian Directory* (London, 1673), pp. 548, 582.

2. *The Office of Christian Parents* (Cambridge, 1616), pp. 73, 74. William Gouge, *Of Domesticall Duties* (London, 1622), pp. 534, 586. Richard Baxter, *The Poor Husbandman's Advocate* (1691), quoted in Richard B. Schlatter, *The Social Ideas of Religious Leaders, 1660–1688* (Oxford, 1940), p. 38. Samuel Willard, *A Complete Body of Divinity* (Boston, 1726), p. 813.

3. Roger Ascham, *The Scholemaster* (London, 1570), ff. 15v–16. Christopher Wase, *Considerations Concerning Free Schools* (Oxford, 1678), pp. 33–34. Thomas Tryon, *Some Memories of the Life* (London, 1705), pp. 14ff. Martin Billingsley, *The Pens Excellencie* (London, 1618), sigs. B4v, Cv. David Brown, *The Introduction to the True Understanding of the Whole Arte of Expedition in Teaching To Write* (London, 1638), sigs. Bv, B4v.

4. David Brown, *The New Invention Instituted Calligraphia* (St. Andrews, 1622), pp. 58–59. Brown, *Introduction to the True Understanding,* sig. B3.

5. Billingsley, *Pens Excellencie,* sigs. B4, C. Thomas Dilworth, *The Schoolmasters Assistant,* 17th ed. (Philadelphia, 1773), p. xix. This popular manual first appeared in London in the 1740s but was based on a tradition which went back to the sixteenth century.

6. Nicholas Breton, *The Court and Country* (London, 1618), in W. H. Dunham and S. Pargellis, eds, *Complaint and reform in England 1436–1714* (New York, 1938), p. 469.

7. Thomas More, *The Apologye* (London, 1533) p. 20–20v. Richard Steele, *The Husbandmans Calling,* 2nd ed. (London, 1672), p. 57. At one extremity of Protestantism there were even those who eschewed the book, preferring to trust in divine illumination and the workings of the spirit. See for example J. De Hoop Scheffer, *History of the Free Churchmen* (Ithaca, New York, 1922), pp. 103–4, 201–6.

8. Henry Conset, *The Practice of the Spiritual or Ecclesiastical Courts* (London,

1685), pp. 116, 117. Charles Sisson, "Marks as signatures," *The Library*, 9 (1928). See also M. G. Guigue, *De l'origine de la signature et de son emploi au moyen age* (Paris, 1863).

9. The quantitative evidence discussed here is derived from ecclesiastical court depositions in the dioceses of London, Norwich, Exeter and Durham, described and evaluated in David Cressy, *Literacy and the Social Order* (Cambridge, 1980), ch. 5.

10. See note 9.

11. Breton, *Court and Country*, p. 468.

12. The distinction is made in Richard Mulcaster, *Positions* (London, 1581), p. 198, and in Edward Chamberlayne, *Angliae Notitia*, 3rd ed. (London, 1669), p. 445.

13. "The last will and testament of me, Robert Keayne," in Boston Record Commissioners, *Tenth Report* (Boston, 1886). The quoted passages are on pp. 39, 41, 42. For a general discussion of this document see Bernard Bailyn, "The *Apologia* of Robert Keayne," *William and Mary Quarterly*, 3rd ser., 7, 4 (1950), pp. 568–87.

14. Schoenbaum, *William Shakespeare, a Documentary Life* (New York, 1975), pp. 30–38. David Cressy, "Jack Cade's Rebels and Shakespeare's Father: Illiteracy in Elizabethan England," paper read at the Renaissance Society of America meeting at U.C.L.A., April 1980.

15. William L. Sache, ed., *The Diary of Roger Lowe* (London, 1938), pp. 14–46. American Antiquarian Society, Ms. Account Book of Dr. John Barton, 1662–76.

16. Examples are cited in Roger Schofield, "The Measurement of Literacy in Pre-industrial England," in Jack Goody, ed., *Literacy in Traditional Societies* (Cambridge, 1968), p. 313; Elizabeth L. Eisenstein, *The Printing Press as an Agent of Change* (Cambridge and New York, 1978), p. 130.

17. Boston Record Commissioners, *Seventh report* (Boston, 1881), pp. 30, 108. Nobody knows if the town criers' books survive.

18. Richard Baxter, *Christian Directory*, p. 60.

19. Details will be found in Francois Furet and Jacques Ozouf, *Lire et ecrire* (Paris, 1977) and Kenneth A. Lockridge, *Literacy in Colonial New England* (New York, 1974).

20. Margaret Spufford, *Contrasting Communities* (Cambridge, 1974), pp. 173, 218.

21. William J. Gilmore, "Elementary Literacy on the Eve of the Industrial Revolution: Trends in Rural New England, 1760–1830," American Antiquarian Society, *Proceedings*, forthcoming.

22. These figures are derived from subscriptions to the Protestation, the Vow and Covenant, and the Solemn League and Covenant, described and evaluated in Cressy, *Literacy and the Social Order*, ch. 4.

23. Cressy, *Literacy and the Social Order*, ch. 5–8.

24. Lockridge, *Literacy in Colonial New England*, pp. 45–6, 83.

25. Egil Johansson, "The History of Literacy in Sweden in Comparison with Some Other Countries," *Education Reports Umea* 12 (1977).

Toward a Cultural Ecology of
Literacy in England, 1600–1850

by Thomas W. Laqueur

Thomas Laqueur, a historian at the University of California, Berkeley, has a strong interest in popular culture and education in England from the six-teenth to the nineteenth centuries. He has explored this area in Religion and Respectability: Sunday Schools and Working Class Culture, 1780–1850 (*New Haven: Yale University Press, 1976*) *and a number of related articles.*

In this essay, he reviews such matters as the availability of schooling and economic incentives, whose role in the spread of literacy in this period may have been exaggerated. Literacy, he argues, was often sought because it helped a threatened traditional culture to defend itself against the new forces of the market.

The historical study of literacy suffers from over a decade of revi-sionism. It was once thought that the industrial revolution cre-ated tens of thousands of new and increasingly technical jobs which required an increasingly educated workforce. Now it ap-pears that literacy rates in the new industrial towns fell through-out the second half of the eighteenth century, and until at least 1850, they remained well below the literacy rates of the compos-ite national average and still further below the average of nonin-dustrial towns of comparable size.[1] Indeed—as the recent experi-ence of Pakistani workers in English industry or Turkish workers in German manufacturing suggests—in order to perform routine factory tasks one need not even know the language of one's host country, much less be able to read or write.

Moreover, literacy does not seem to be correlated with mod-ernity as modernization theorists once thought; a higher percent-age of people could read and write in eighteenth-century North-umberland, Cumberland, and Westmoreland—the dark corners of the realm—than in any other region of the country excepting the Metropolis. Nor do literacy and the "modern personality" appear to be correlated. Even by the end of the nineteenth century, literacy had not outstripped the importance of various ascriptive characteristics as determinants of mobility.[2] More generally, the role of education in social mobility is being called into question.[3] In short, literacy seems reduced to one of those historical phenomena which are studied because they are there; neither theoretical nor practical considerations render it important.

The absence of such considerations, in this era of disillusionment with modernization theory, is due in part to a lack of systematic data about which to theorize and in part to the bankruptcy of old questions. We know overall literacy rates and differential rates of literacy for various groups in society, for this or that locale, from the sixteenth through the nineteenth century. But few plausible hypotheses of the middle range can be suggested, much less explored, without the data, not just on literacy but on social structure. Such data, from a wide variety of English parishes, will soon be provided by the Cambridge Group.

Yet myth that literacy might well be and ignorant as we are of its social and geographic distribution, it remains at the core of a constellation of compelling, disparate yet interrelated questions in the politico-cultural history of England. An increasingly large proportion of quite ordinary men and women in England, in sharp contrast to those in Ireland or in large parts of France or Italy or most certainly Russia, learned to read, and a somewhat smaller number to write, beginning in the early sixteenth century and continuing on to the late nineteenth century.[4]

Why and how? Why was it that the eighteen families in the tiny Yorkshire Parish of Braythorp without aid from endowments or charities supported "a poor woman [that] teaches children to read English"? Why was there somehow "a petty schoolmaster or School-dame who taught children to read English and write at so much per quarter" in each village of the parish of Felix Kirk with its 189 families?[5] If, as I will argue, there was no shortage of elementary education in England before the era of government grants or school societies, why was everyone not literate? Or conversely, why were some literate and others not? And why so many more men than women?

The problem, however, is not simply how and why people become literate. It is rather why the printed word in its various forms assumes significance in the lives of individuals and societies. Perhaps the most prevalent icon of late eighteenth- and early nineteenth-century radicalism was the printing press; "rude mechanic preachers" were frequently caricatured waving a book, and the frontispiece of the most oft reprinted text in the English tradition, Bunyan's *Pilgrim's Progress,* shows Christian setting out on his journey, Bible in hand. Manifestations of the written and the printed word abound in the nooks and crannies of English society during the eighteenth century. From chapbooks and notices of cattle diseases, to anonymous threatening letters and coffee house newspapers, from placards to prisoners' protests to paupers' appeals to magistrates, the word was everywhere.

The meaning of literacy, of its growth and social distribution can only be understood in its broadest cultural context. For most people before the mid-nineteenth century, literacy was not the inevitable product of schooling; nor was non-literacy a necessary consequence of its absence. Literacy was not simply a response to economic necessity, or the opportunity for social mobility. It was in large measure a consumption good which, as Mary Douglas has argued more generally, makes "visible or stable the categories of culture." The main object of the consumer, she argues, "can only be to construct an intelligible universe with the goods he choose." [6] If this is true and if literacy can be regarded as a consumer good, then the historical study of literacy must be a study of the interrelationship of reading and writing with culture; it must be essentially a study in cultural ecology.

Advances in ecology, however, are in large measure dependent on a thorough knowledge of the distribution in space and time of the flora and fauna under consideration. Unfortunately, we will have no such knowledge regarding literacy until we have the Cambridge Group's data. On the other hand, we do know and have known since W. L. Sargent's survey in 1867 that over 60 percent of men and 36 percent of women in England could sign their names by the mid-eighteenth century, that women's ability to write their names improved steadily, reaching 42 percent by 1800 and 52 percent by the mid-1840s, and that men's ability to write increased little until the early nineteenth century and then improved from around 60 percent in 1815 to almost 70 percent by 1845.[7]

We also know that more people could read, if only a little, than could write. By the nineteenth century in Ramsbottom, a Lancashire cotton town, only 26.5 percent or 531 of those surveyed could write, but 1,316 or 66 percent could read. Among adults in Pendleton, 5,924 out of 8,878 adults questioned, i.e., 66 percent, could not write, but only 2,653, i.e., 30 percent, could not read. In three Rutland parishes the results are similar: 61 percent of 483 adults could write, but 92 percent could read. The relationship between the ability to read and to write varied from place to place and between sexes, although we know very little about such variations. Nevertheless, it remains clear that by the middle of the eighteenth century, when over half the population of England could write a little, quite probably another 20–30 percent could read at some level.[8]

Our knowledge of the history of literacy before the systematic registration of marriages in 1754 is much less secure. I disagree with David Cressy that the evidence is such that we can identify the ups and downs of sixteenth-, seventeenth-, and early eighteenth-century literacy rates.[9] Our samples are too small and we know too little about the populations from which they were drawn for such an exercise to be useful. But the educated conjectures published by Stone in 1969 regarding general trends have not been essentially altered. Literacy, as measured by the ability to sign one's name, grew from 25–30 percent of males in 1600 to twice that proportion a century and a half later.

We also know that literacy was not evenly distributed in the population. Those farther up the social scale were more likely to be able to read and write than those farther down. Men were more literate than women. Urban literacy was higher than literacy in the countryside in the mid-eighteenth century, though the deteriorating situation in new, especially industrial areas closed this gap by 1800. Finally, we know something of the geographical distribution of literacy by 1840. It was highest in London and in the extreme north—Cumberland, Northumberland, and Westmoreland—and it was lowest in southern agricultural counties and in the industrial counties of Lancashire, Staffordshire, Worcestershire, and the West Riding.[10] This, in rough outline, is what we are in a position to study about literacy.

Our first moves toward a cultural ecology of literacy thus cannot be overly subtle. We must first persuade ourselves that the ability to read and write is not simply the product of economic necessity or the inevitable product of schools and formal education. The history of literacy is not an epiphenomenon of the history of the marketplace or the classroom.

Evidence from other societies suggests that quite complicated economic transactions are possible without use of the written word. Moreover, until quite recently, only a tiny proportion of the workforce needed, in some absolute sense, to be literate. If, as David Cressy showed, 60 percent of artisans and tradesmen in early seventeenth-century Norwich were illiterate, it is difficult to argue that the remaining 40 percent required literacy for their work.[11] No argument from necessity can account for the fact that 82 percent of joiners and carpenters could write in the Lancashire of the 1830s, but only 55 percent of foundrymen and iron or brass moulders. Why should 70 percent of shoemakers be literate but less than 50 percent of hatters?[12] Cultural factors and not some ironclad external constraint lie behind these variations.

There are three major difficulties with the argument that literacy is primarily the result of schooling and that differential rates of literacy over time, between several groups, or in different places, are the results of differential access to formal education. It assumes that the prevalence of schooling is determined independently of rates of literacy; in other words, that schooling is an exogenous variable. Moreover, it fails to take into account the inappropriateness of our institutional category "school" to most of the teaching situations of the early modern period; and finally, it falsely presumes that most relevant education took place in a school, however loosely described, and that a person's educational attainments were dependent on the amount of time spent in such an institution during childhood.

Before 1876, school attendance in England was entirely voluntary. Not until the 1840s was the majority of students attending institutions provided by some outside agency, and even these students in many cases had to pay some fees. One hundred years earlier no more than 20–30 percent of all those enrolled were in schools provided by anything other than private venture. Thus, the greater part of schooling for all of the period we are considering was created by the same forces that created literacy; both are products of deeper cultural currents, and the latter cannot be explained in terms of the former.[13]

Moreover, even when available schooling is treated as an exogenous variable, it seems to have little effect on the literacy rates. If we consider the most literate counties in England, only in Westmoreland was the proportion of students taught free in endowed or nonendowed schools, i.e., 54 percent, above the national average of 49 percent; in Cumberland, on the other hand, only 38 percent were taught free and in Northumberland only 28 percent, both considerably below the average for England as a whole. Attendance at schools was, to be sure, considerably above the national average, but this reflects the choice of parents, not the provision of schools.[14] One could also point to the fact that in the northern counties literacy was almost as high as in 1839 without any government involvement in education as it was in Scotland, where the much-vaunted parochial system provided for 31 percent of children in tax-supported schools. In short, some complex cultural constellation and not the exogenous provision of elementary education fueled the high literacy rates north and just south of the river Tweed.

Comparisons such as these on the county level are notoriously suspect, but attempts to correlate literacy and schooling on a parish level run afoul of closely related evidentiary and conceptual difficulties. We know very little about how much education was available in preindustrial England because the categories of "school" and of "teacher" were not yet as distinct as they became by the time of the great nineteenth-century parliamentary investigation. Thus, as Alan Smith points out, women who taught reading and occasionally writing are absent entirely from the records of the Diocese of Lichfield, except when recusancy or some other failing brought them to ecclesiastical attention.[15] Men and women not licensed as teachers appear here and there in records which have nothing to do with education; a man presented as a fornicator turns out be a teacher as well; another man got into trouble for being a Presbyterian and he too, the record reveals, taught.[16]

Being a schoolmaster or schoolmistress was for many only one of several possible designations of occupational status. Most seventeenth- and eighteenth-century visitation queries ask only about endowed and charity schools and those who taught in them. Allusions to other teaching was purely coincidental. The 1764 Visitation Returns of the Archbishopric of York reveal, for example, that among the twenty families in Firbeck there was no school of the sort inquired after, but there was "one small private school taught by a woman"; "no charity School or Publick School of any sort" in Elloughton, "except a Teaching mistress and she uncertain number [i.e., she does not know how many children are being taught];" in Abberford we come upon Elizabeth Gill Spinster and Francis Harber, papists, who keep petty schools; in Narby Marsh a "sober man" teaches; in Eggton Chapel there was no endowed school, but "several Petty Schools taught by Poor People." We learn from a trial for spousal support in 1820 that in 1798 a carpenter of Salisbury abandoned his pregnant wife and ran off to London. Bereft, she started a school and taught for her subsistence until she had saved enough to go to London, where she worked in a linenworks. Or how about Wilfrid Thomas, clockmaker and keeper of a day school in Hotham, York? Men and women like these only randomly appear in the surveys upon which historians rely. Poor people, spinsters, fornicators, recusants, Presbyterians, a sober man, a well-meaning person, a clockmaker, an old woman, an abandoned wife—these are the "schools" of the eighteenth century, and these are impossible to quantify as the independent variable of a regression analysis.[17]

I conclude from this evidence and from the work on educational provision by Margaret Spufford, David Cressy, Alan Smith, and others that England by the seventeenth century was sufficiently literate to produce in almost every parish a person able to teach reading and writing should a local demand exist.[18] "Schooling," in itself an inappropriate category for much of the instruction offered before the nineteenth century, was thus in ready supply, called into being by the demand for literacy. The spread of literacy over time and down the social scale was constrained not by the absence of teachers and schools but by the absence of a cultural context in which literacy mattered.

This is not to suggest, however, that poverty and other material constraints did not seriously circumscribe the education opportunity for the great majority of English boys and girls well into this century. Yet, the acquisition of basic literacy before the last quarter of the nineteenth century was not the result of a single period of childhood schooling but of a more informal and protracted process which could continue well into adolescence and even adulthood.

Evidence from nineteenth-century surveys, from earlier individual biographies, and from contemporary studies of the third world suggest that childhood schooling was only one way, not itself sufficient and in some cases not necessary, to become literate. Work alternated with formal and informal education until at least young adulthood and more generally the demarcation between living and learning was not as distinct as it became later.

Statistics of education from Pendleton and from Kingston on Hull collected around 1840 are suggestive on this point. In these towns investigators sought to ascertain educational achievement at different ages and for various degrees of schooling by going house to house and interviewing parents, children, or both. It is striking that the oldest group of children showed consistently higher levels of attainment independent of additional schooling. In Kingston, 6.2 percent of 3397 children, aged 5 to 10, whose skills were ascertained could write, 34.8 percent of the 2879 children aged 15–21 could write. Yet less than 2 percent (42), of this last group were in school, less than 5 percent had attended school until they had reached thirteen, and 55 percent had left by their eleventh birthday. In Pendleton the contrast between age groups is not so striking for reasons that are at present obscure. Nevertheless, in this textile town 99 out of 581, i.e., 10.5 percent of children 5 to 10 could write, 278 out of 887, i.e., 32 percent of those aged 10–15 could write, and 250 out of 612, i.e., 41 percent of those 15–20 could write.[19] Clearly learning continued even after schooling of an intermittent nature had ceased.

Working class autobiographies from the eighteenth and early nineteenth century reinforce the impression that schooling was only one part of an extended process of elementary education. Take the case of James Lackington, born in 1746, son of a Wellington shoemaker. James was sent to an old woman to learn to read when he was five and remained in her school on and off for two or three years. He sold pies for the ensuing six years and worked occasionally for his father until at age 14½ he was apprenticed to a Baptist shoemaker. In his new position he became interested in religious controversy and paid his mistress and his master's youngest son to tutor him in reading and spelling so that he might more intelligently take sides in the debate.[20]

William Hutton, the antiquarian, provides another example. Born in 1723, he was sent to dame school at the usual age of five. Two years later he quit to work in a silk mill. Then when he was thirteen he began taking lessons anew from an old woman named Gell who happened to be lodging with his family. Or consider the London journalist James Hone, whose education is very similar to that reported by his fellow radical Francis Place. Hone learned the alphabet and reading from his father; his family, like most at the time, owned a Bible which served as the text. He went to a dame school when he was six and at age seven began at a more advanced boys' school. But, within three months, he developed smallpox and withdrew. For the next four years his father provided what education he received; at age eleven he went back to school again, but after a short time got involved in a fight with a fellow student and, when the master sided with his opponent, quit formal education for good. Some never went to school and yet learned to read. A woman in Pendleton told investigators that "I took larning up o' mysel, when I went to a printing shop [calico-printers] and a mon tout me, and then I bout up histories and books as was mie reading." [21]

The pattern in the countryside was probably not very different, except that schooling followed more closely the troughs of the yearly cycle of planting, cultivation, rest, harvest, rest. Consider John Clare, the poet, born in a Northamptonshire fen border village of parents themselves barely able to read. Their house, nevertheless, had a Bible and a few chapbooks. Every year, until he was eleven or twelve, John went to school for three months or so. First, as was usual, to a dame and then to a master more distant from his home. He would practice writing at home during the long intervals between more formal education.[22]

Examples could be multiplied but all the evidence suggests that well into the nineteenth century children went to school "when they could be spared" and that schooling was not the regular and continuous process it has become today. Thus, the means of acquiring basic skills were widely diffused, and the question for the historian is why in some places rather than others, more among men than among women, people did or did not choose to participate more immediately in literate culture. Why, for example, amongst the Northumbrian peasantry, was there "no greater stigma" that could be attached to parents "than that of leaving their children without the means of ordinary education"? What made the northern counties a "society where . . . intelligence is held in estimation"? [23]

Our problem, in short, is understanding the formation of a literate culture, the making of a world in which it means something to be able to read and write. In some measure, the making of this world involves the dissemination of the printed word. Again, our knowledge is extremely limited and we have no idea of the geography or the temporal sequence of the spread of books and other literature. But evidence is accumulating to suggest an extraordinary penetration of print into all levels of society beginning in the late sixteenth century and continuing into the nineteenth century. My research has found that in three sets of inventories, ranging from the middle of the sixteenth to the end of the seventeenth century, between 14 and 22 percent of the deceased are listed as owning books. Since books were of relatively small value, and since they were often classed with miscellaneous junk—"old clothes and other items"—we have reason to believe that these figures underestimate levels of book ownership. My work does not enable one to draw conclusions about the growth of book ownership, although it may be significant that the lowest percentage of inventories with books was derived from a set limited to the early seventeenth century. [24]

Peter Clark's work on book ownership in Kent shows an unmistakable trend toward wider dissemination of print during the late sixteenth and early seventeenth centuries. Among male townsmen in Canterbury, 8 percent owned books in the 1560s, 33–34 percent around 1600, 45–46 percent in the 1620s and 1630s; in Faversham 15 percent of inventories listed books in 1560, 32–41 percent in the 1590s and 1600s, and 40–49 percent in the 1620s and 1630s, respectively. The trend was similar in Maidstone. In short, by 1640, at least 40 percent of those whose property was inventoried owned books. One wonders into how many more houses the ten thousand titles or what we now call the Thomason Tracts brought print during the revolutionary decades.[25]

By the late 1830s and early 1840s, books, if only the Bible, were far more widely dispersed. "Few dwellings," we are told, were entirely without books in three Rutlandshire parishes; 94 percent of the 209 families in an agricultural parish in Bedfordshire owned at least a Bible; 96 percent of 344 working class homes (mostly those of weavers) in Norwich; 85 percent of the working class houses in West Bromich; 81 percent in Miles Plating, a model working class section of Manchester; and 73 percent in Bristol contained a Bible or other literature.[26]

There is little point in rehearsing once again the history of classics like the *Pilgrim's Progress,* which went through at least 160 editions between 1678 and 1792, and was sufficiently popular to warrant printing in sixteen provincial centers in addition to London. Nor need one point out the vast traffic in chapbooks, which reached even someone like John Clare's semi-literate father, who bought the "superstitious ballad tales that are hawked about the street for a penny." Nor need one point out again the spread of newspapers in eighteenth-century England, of coffee houses—2000 in London alone by the early eighteenth century, it has been suggested—of a swelling tide of governmental forms, announcements, and questionnaires.[27] The evidence from publishing suggests that there was no shortage of print in England before factories and school societies.

It is important, however, to explore more intensely the social and cultural contexts of reading, of writing, and of print. Again, systematic evidence relating literacy to the religious or political life of a community or to its social structure is lacking. We do, however, have qualitative and scattered evidence which suggests that religion, politics, and social standing affected the cultural ambiance in which individuals lived and thus the meaning of literacy in their lives.

In Holland, recent work has shown there was a systematic variation in the literacy of Protestants and Catholics, in nine rural Utrecht parishes from 1580 to 1800, across all social categories. While differences were slight amongst highly literate categories—notables, clergy, bureaucrats, and upper tradesmen—they were far more striking lower down the scale. Fifty-one percent of Protestant laborers but only 37 percent of Catholics could sign their names.[28] Although the absolute rates varied over the period, the differentials remained throughout. The reasons for these differences are complicated but suggest that there might still be life in the old adage that Protestantism is the religion of the book.

In the English case, one would like to know the impact of Puritanism, or later of evangelical dissent, on literacy. How many times was the early nineteenth-century story of this old man repeated in the centuries before?

> I geet no schooling when I wur a lad, but arter I wur married I geed amongst religious folk at Tinley, and geet a bit o' neet schooling; so I can read i' th' Testament. I mean to have another stir at it this summer.[29]

Opponents of mass literacy associated evangelicalism with reading and reading, in turn, with at least the potential for radicalism. Davies Giddy in opposing a prohibition on bull baiting argued in 1801 that Methodism, though itself not Jacobin, led to reading and reading to Tom Paine and seditious literature to sedition. Rather than encouraging the working class to sit indoors with books, they should be encouraged to engage in the old sports; "show me a radical who is a bull baiter," he challenged his opponents.

Qualitative evidence from the birth of evangelicalism in the mid-eighteenth century through the autobiographies of primitive Methodists in the mid-nineteenth, attests to the importance of a religious motive to literacy, or put differently, argues for the increased cultural significance of literacy in particular religious settings. Precisely how important religion was in determining overall literacy levels or in affecting the differential between men and women remains to be discovered.

Politics and literacy too were closely interdependent, though specifying the relationship will be difficult. England was an intensely political nation during the eighteenth century, which encompassed, if only sporadically, an increasingly wide swath of the population. The written word bound together political culture at all levels. At its upper reaches this is obvious; one need only survey the huge literature on faction and party, of arguments for this or that fiscal, military, or social policy. But written communication affected more popular politics as well. A Birmingham gentleman wrote to one of the secretaries of state in 1721 that "last Saturday's Paper is now become the General talk not only of this Place, but Coventry, Warwick, etc. In every Alehouse People have the London journal in their Hands, shewing to each other with a kind of joy the most audacious Reflections therein contained." [30] By the time of Wilkes the stream had grown to a river and by the early nineteenth century to a torrent. In 1820 the Home Office got word of numbers of peddlers who supported themselves as they criss-crossed the country, bringing pro-Queen Caroline literature into the tiniest villages and hamlets.

I do not want to suggest, however, that literacy was tied exclusively to the more "modern" institutionally based working class politics of the 1790s onward, though its political world was intimately connected with the press and its culture was self-consciously literate. Defensive politics, the politics of the moral economy, of the opposition to the marketplace, was also mediated through writing and reading. As Edward Thompson has pointed out, "the letter or handbill was well understood by both parties in the market conflict, as one element within a regular and ritualized code of behaviour." A letter such as

> This is to give Notis to badgers and fore Stallers of grain that there as Been sum in perticular a woceing your Motions and there whill Be in a wicks time some men Com ought of the Colepits by Night to Meak fire brans of all the abitations of the forestallers of grain.[31]

may be less than orthographically correct or consistent, but it leaves the political function of such literate communication beyond doubt.

The history of literacy and the history of political culture are profoundly interconnected. An anti-Jacobin pamphlet in which the working class hero teaches his elderly mother to read so that she may find comfort in scripture or a Jacobin tobacco paper printed with

> 1 am p.uzz.led ho?
> w. Tolivew hil:ek inG.C.R.
> aft mA.Ya bus E my.
> R—i G—ht
> SAND TAX! the. JOY,—so.F!
> DAY.

distributed to guests at a pub, were possible only in a literate society and one whose political culture in turn generated increased literacy.[32]

I want finally to draw our attention briefly to the effect of changes in social structure and mobility on literacy. If literacy rates are in some measure dependent on the cultural expectation of particular groups or the cultural milieu of particular settings, we need to study the rise and fall of such groups and such settings. Thus we might explore systematically the idea that the comparatively high literacy rate of towns like Preston or Oxford in 1750, in which only 28 percent and 23 percent of men respectively could not sign their names, compared to 40 percent in the country as a whole, are due to the growth of traditionally more literate service and marketing trades associated with what Peter Borsay termed the urban renaissance of the eighteenth century.[33] The slow secular growth of literacy from the sixteenth through the early nineteenth century may in part be due to the expansion of generally more literate strata of societies and the growth of the usually more literate centers during the period. But of course not all urban areas remained more literate than the national average. Lancashire cotton towns experienced a downward trend during the late eighteenth century and then, surprisingly, just when the adverse social effects of the first industrial revolution were at their most painful, began to improve.[34]

We need more careful studies which will establish the parameters of rise or fall of literacy in different kinds of cities. We also need detailed local work on the effect of changing economic structures on literacy. What, for example, happened to female literacy in Corfe Castle, where between 1790 and 1850 the opportunities for girls' and women's labour dropped drastically; how does it compare to Cardington where such opportunities remained high?[35] We need to understand more about the role of London, and more generally of geographical mobility, in the creation of a literate society. As much as a sixth of the population of the country passed some time in their lives in the metropolis; they may have entered as illiterate countrymen and left as literate return migrants.

I have argued in this paper that literacy must be seen as the product not simply of schooling or of opportunities for elementary education, but as the result of a culturally defined need to be able to read or write. A theory of literacy and I think of education generally must be in large measure a theory of the meaning of what is learned in the lives of boys and girls, men and women. This paper suggests that the detailed empirical work that needs to be done must be informed by such considerations.

Notes

1. See Michael Sanderson, "Literacy and Social Mobility in the Industrial Revolution in England," *Past and Present* 56 (August 1972) and my reply along with his rejoinder in *Past and Present* 64 (August 1974), pp. 96–112.

2. This point is argued extensively in Harvey J. Graff, *The Literacy Myth* (New York: Academic Press, 1979), esp. ch. 2–4.

3. The importance of education in determining social mobility is, of course, a large and vexing question. On its relative unimportance, see Christopher Jencks, et al., *Inequality*, which in turn generated its own extensive literature.

4. For England I rely on R.S. Schofield, "Dimensions of Illiteracy, 1750–1850," *Explorations in Economic History*

10 (1973): 4, esp. pp. 444 and 447; and on Lawrence Stone, "Literacy and Education in England, 1640–1900" *Past and Present* 42 (1968).

5. These examples are drawn from the Archdiocese of York Visitation Returns, Borthwick Institute, York, MS BP 1764, vol. 1–14, MFB 43–46.

6. Mary Douglas, *The World of Goods* (New York: Basic Books, 1979), pp. 59 and ff.

7. See William L. Sargent, "On the Progress of Elementary Education," *Journal of the Royal Statistical Society* (JRSS), vol. 30, pt. 1, March 1867, and note 4 above.

8. R. S. Schofield discusses the relationship of the ability to read to the ability to write in "The Measurement of Literacy on Pre-Industrial England," Jack Goody, ed., *Literacy in Traditional Societies* (Cambridge, 1968); for Ramsbottom see "Statistics of the Parish of Ramsbottom" by P. M. M'Dougal in *JRSS*, vol. 1, January 1839, p. 539; for Pendleton see "Report on the State of Education in Pendleton" by the Statistical Society of Manchester, *JRSS*, vol. 2, March 1839, p., 80; for Rutland, see "Report on the Condition of the Population in Three Parishes in Rutlandshire," in March 1839, *JRSS*, vol. 2, March 1839, p. 299.

9. I refer to the data presented by Professor Cressy in "Educational Opportunity in Tudor and Stuart England," *History of Education Quarterly*, Fall 1976, esp., pp, 315–16 and "Literacy in Seventeenth-Century England: More Evidence," *Journal of Interdisciplinary History* 8 (Summer 1977), esp. 146–50.

10. See Sargent, "Elementary Education," tables R and S.

11. Cressy, "Literacy," p. 150.

12. Sanderson, "Literacy," p. 90.

13. See T. Laqueur, "Working Class Demand and the Growth of English Elementary Eduction," in L. Stone, ed., *Schooling and Society* (Baltimore:

Johns Hopkins Press, 1976), esp. pp. 192; 202–3.

14. Calculated from "A Table, showing the proportion of scholars who are educated gratuitously, and those who pay for their instruction . . .," PP 1820 (177), 12:346–47.

15. Alan Smith, "Private Schools and Schoolmasters in the Diocese of Lichfield and Coventry in the Seventeenth Century," *History of Education*, 1975, 5:2, p. 125.

16. Peyton, S.A., ed., *The Churchwardens' Presentments in the Oxfordshire Peculiars of Dorchester, Thame, and Danbury,* Oxfordshire Record Society Series, vol. 10, 1928, pp. 257–58.

17. See note 5 for Yorkshire; *London Courier,* July 8, 1820, p. 4; W.P. Baker, *Parish Registers and Illiteracy in East Yorkshire* (East Yorkshire Local History Society, 1961), p. 29.

18. I am thinking especially of Margaret Spufford's "The Schooling of the Peasantry in Cambridgeshire, 1575–1700" in Joan Thirsk, ed., *Land, Church, and People* (Reading, Berks, 1970).

19. "Report on the State of Education in the Borough of Kingston-upon-Hull" by the Manchester Statistical Society, *JRSS*, vol. 4, July 1841, esp. table 8; for Pendleton see *JRSS*, vol. 2, March 1839, esp. Table 9, p. 82.

20. *Memoirs of the Forty-Five First Years of the Life of James Lackington . . . Written by Himself* (London, 1830), p. 56 and pp. 32–57 more generally.

21. *The Life of William Hutton . . . Written by Himself* (London, 1816), p. 22, and pp. 1–24 generally; F. W. Hackwood, *William Hone* (London, 1912), pp. 24–25.

22. E. Blunden, ed., *Sketches in the Life of John Clare written by Himself* (London, 1931), pp. 46–49.

23. L. Hindmarsh, "On the State of Agriculture and Condition of the Agricultural Labourers of the Northern Di-

vision of Northumberland, *JRSS*, November 1838, p. 414.

24. T. Laqueur, "The Cultural Origins of Popular Literacy in England 1500-1850," *Oxford Review of Education*, vol. 2, no. 3, 1976, p. 264.

25. Peter Clark, "The Ownership of Books in England, 1560-1640," in Stone, ed., *Schooling*, p. 99.

26. *JRSS*, vol. 2, October 1839, p. 299; John Edward Martin, "Statistics of an Agricultural Parish in Bedfordshire," *JRSS*, vol. 6, August 1843, p. 253; "Moral Statistics of a Section of the City of Norwich," *JRSS*, vol. 1, January 1839, p. 540; "Report on the State of Education Among the Working Classes in the Parish Of West Bromwich," *JRSS*, October 1839, p. 377; "State of 176 Families in Miles Platting," *JRSS*, vol. 1, May 1838, p. 36; C. B. Fripp, "Report on the Condition of the Working Classes in Bristol," *JRSS*, vol. 2, October 1839, p. 371.

27. For Bunyan see F. M. Harrison, "Editions of the *Pilgrim's Progress*," *The Library*, NS 2, 1901, pp. 242-59; regarding coffeehouses see Aytoun Ellis, *The Penny Universities, A History of Coffee-Houses* (London, 1956), p. XIV.

28. E. P. deBooy, *De Weldaet der Scholen* (Utrecht, n.d.), esp. table 2b, p. 327.

29. *JRSS*, March 1839, p. 70.

30. *State Papers Domestic* 35, vol. 28 (15), cited in James R. Sutherland, "The Circulation of Newspapers and Literary Periodicals, 1700-30," *The Library*, Ser. 4, no. 15, 1935, p. 118.

31. E. P. Thompson, "The Crime of Anonymity," in D. Hey, et al., ed., *Albion's Fatal Tree*, (1975) pp. 279-80.

32. John Money, *Experience and Identity, Birmingham and the West Midlands 1760-1800* (Manchester: UP, 1977), p. 155. The quotation is from BM, Add MS 16922, f. 13 and is a phonetic spelling of "I am puzzled how to live while kingcraft may abuse my rights and tax the joys of day."

33. Peter Borsay, "The English Urban Renaissance: The Development of Provincial Urban Culture ca. 1680-1760," *Social History* 5, May 1977. Jan De Vries has shown that in the latter part of the eighteenth century there was significant growth of urban areas in general and disproportionately rapid growth in smaller cities. He feels that these trends probably began earlier in England than in the remainder of Western Europe. See "Patterns of Urbanization in Pre-Industrial Europe, 1500-1800," unpublished MS and personal conversations. Peter Wrigley found a growth of the service sector in Colyton from 1609-12 to 1765-70 from 3 percent to 8 percent of those employed; by 1851 13 percent were so employed. See *Local Population Studies*, no. 18, 1977.

34. For Lancashire cotton towns, see Sanderson, "Literacy . . ." and Laqueur, "Literacy . . ." in *Past and Present*, nos. 56 and 64 respectively. It is also important to remember that we know almost nothing about the effect of changes in the ethnic composition of cities on literacy rates. One might well imagine that the influx of unskilled Irish workers into the industrial towns of Lancashire lowered the levels of literacy in these locations. On the other hand, such assertions may be pure prejudice on the part of the historian, picked up from contemporary observers.

35. Studies like Osamu Saito's "Who Worked When," *LPS*, no. 22, 1979, need to be integrated with studies of literacy.

Illiterate Americans and Nineteenth-Century Courts: The Meanings of Literacy

by Edward Stevens

Edward Stevens is professor of education at Ohio University. His recent book, with Lee Soltow, The Rise of Literacy and the Common School in the United States *(Chicago: University of Chicago Press, 1981), draws on sources as diverse as wills, census records, school attendance, book ownership, and pedagogy to describe the growth of American literacy from the colonial period to 1870.*

In this paper, Professor Stevens examines the position of the illiterate person before the courts during the nineteenth century, as witness, party to contracts, and juror. By the end of the century, he argues, the illiterate person had come to suffer certain disabilities, expressed especially in litigation over contracts, which dimmed his prospects for justice and left his position increasingly untenable in a free market economy.

This essay studies the problem of the meanings of literacy and the consequences of those meanings by bringing to bear on the problem the relatively unexploited data base or case law. Because law itself is a pervasive context for human behavior, the use of case law makes it possible not only to study the meanings of literacy, but also to analyze those meanings within specific behavioral contexts. Law, as Haskins has explained, is "not merely a complex of rules and procedures for the settlement of controversies"; it is, rather, "a means of classifying and bringing into order a vast mass of human relations, and it is these human relations that constitute much of the stuff of which history is made." [1] Similarly, Hurst has noted that law has "entered into the order or individual lives, as well as that of institutions," and the formal records of the law have themselves helped to shape the experience of participants in the legal process.[2] Nowhere is this situation more evident than with the illiterate person whose experiences were limited by his inability to decipher print.

Illiteracy, though no crime itself, often has been a relevant factor in deciding a legal issue, and case law permits us to study the problematic situations in which illiterates find themselves relative to the legal structure. Moreover, statutory changes, departures from and adherence to precedents found in the courts' decisions, in turn, reflect changing social conditions and provide a useful context for assessing the meanings of literacy. Literacy skills and the consequences of their absence may be analyzed for individuals as they deal, for example, with a broad range of contractual relationships, will-making and the signing of deeds, banking and checking, jury duty, workman's compensation, and voting. Thus, we are able, using such cases, to assess the function of literacy within specific contexts of behavior, and to observe, as well, the perceptions of judicial and legal authorities on the condition of the illiterate person. The point might be illustrated in the recent case of *Mills* v. *Lynch* (1963), where the preservation of the illiterate's contractual rights was at stake and the difficulties associated with being illiterate might be decisive. The case, not unusually, involved an illiterate plaintiff John Mills of Randolph County, North Carolina, who had "only a fourth grade education and could not read." Mills was a victim of fraud and misrepresentation in the signing of a deed in trust. Thinking he had signed a deed in trust, Mills unwittingly had actually conveyed his land (eighteen acres) to one Mr. Lynch. Mills had done this at the advice of his lawyer and had not realized his predicament until he attempted to cut and sell timber from "his" land. He then discovered that he had in fact deeded away his land. The court, fortunately for Mills, recognized the misrepresentation which had occurred because Mills could not read the document, and found in Mills's behalf.[3]

In discussing court cases from the nineteenth century, I first focus on the degree to which the illiterate person might properly be called "marginal" in his relationship to the social mainstream.[4] Cases involving the legitimacy of the mark, illiterate witnesses, and juror competency are used to examine the concept of marginality. I do not deal with marginality as it relates to suffrage, since this topic itself would require a separate essay. Secondly, I deal with the problematic relationships of illiterates to contractual agreements. In the first of these concerns, the position taken is contrary to a current assumption that illiterates are bona fide marginal people. Instead, it is hypothesized that the marginality of the illiterate person is a function of social values which have been incorporated into the legislative and judicial process; thus, marginality will be functionally differentiated according to the behavioral contexts for illiteracy. In dealing with the contractual relations involving illiterates, the hypothesis is offered that in the matter of illiterates' behavior in making contracts, the trend away from a contract theory dominated by the concept of equity in the eighteenth century toward a modern "will" theory of contract law in the nineteenth century increasingly put the illiterate person at a disadvantage relative to the literate person.[5]

Illiteracy and the Marginal Person

In discussing the concept of marginality it is important to understand, first, the degree to which the "mark" was considered legitimate (as having authority) to express the intent of the marker. Second, the presumed link between illiteracy and (in)competency must be examined. Presumably, if illiterate witnesses, for instance, were consistently declared incompetent by virtue of their illiteracy, then they would effectively be excluded from this important dimension of civic behavior. Similarly, the legitimacy of the mark would be crucial to the settling of an estate or the transferring of property by deed.

At one level, the authority of the mark is evidenced simply in the number of wills and deeds recorded in court houses and signed with a mark. At another level, however, the question is not so simple and becomes one of asking whether the efficacy of the marker's intent was jeopardized by the condition of being illiterate. As early as 1582 in Great Britain the case of *Thoroughgood* v. *Cole* set forth the principles for judging whether deeds or wills signed with a mark were valid. These were reaffirmed in Shulter's case in 1655 and later compiled by Blackstone.[6] Thoroughgood's case was an action in trespass which had resulted from the signing of a deed by the unlettered Thoroughgood. The case is often cited (it was cited at length in the case of *Pimpinello* v. *Swift and Company* (1930)) because of its great importance in the history of contract law, but its discussion of illiteracy made it, also, a frequent precedent for later cases involving illiterate or blind testators. The principles laid down in *Thoroughgood* were as follows:

> . . . held, 1st, that a deed executed by an illiterate person does not bind him, if read falsely either by the grantee or a stranger; 2ndly, that an illiterate man need not execute a deed before it be read to him in a language which he understands; but if the party executes without desiring it to be

read, the deed is binding; 3rdly, that if an illiterate man execute a deed which is falsely read, or the sense declared differently from the truth, it does not bind him; and that though it be a friend of his, unless there be covin.[7]

Because the state reporter systems were a product of nineteenth century legal record keeping, court records from colonial America do not allow us generally to evaluate the extent to which the legitimacy of the mark was an issue in that period. Undoubtedly, the same issues raised in Thoroughgood's case and Shulter's case were raised in colonial courts. What is clear from colonial records, however, is that illiterate persons, far from being marginal, were frequent participants in a broad range of economic, political, and civic behaviors. Illiterates were frequently parties to contractual relations, and political and civil participation by the unlettered may be observed in a number of instances, including township settlement, petitions, elections, jury duty, and trial testimony. It was not uncommon to find illiterate jurors, and counts of markers for Maryland, Delaware, and New Plymouth during the colonial period show the proportion of illiterate jurors in the late seventeenth century ranging from 11 to 67 percent. Illiterate witnesses were found in a variety of cases involving criminal activity, debts, and land disputes. In Suffolk County, Massachusetts, in 1673, we find the interesting situation of two illiterate persons giving evidence in a case involving the "unjust selling and disposing of several parcels of goods." Ironically, the illiterates testified to the accuracy of an accounting of goods.[8]

During the nineteenth century a number of cases were heard in which the authority or legitimacy of the mark was questioned and the competency of illiterate markers discussed. These cases usually involved disputed wills and deeds and illustrate the dependency of the illiterate persons. Consistently, however, they do reaffirm that the mark had the authority of the law behind it; yet repeatedly, justices also warn of the difficulties associated with using the mark. A British case of 1803 clearly upholds the authority of the mark made by witnesses when attesting to the authenticity of a will. In the opinion given in *Harrison* v. *Harrison* (1803), Lord Chancellor Eldon refers to an earlier case of 1710 which he had located in a notebook of one of his predecessors. He notes of *Gurney* v. *Corbett* (1710), a case heard in the Court of Common Pleas, that there may have been a "great deal of argument" at the time, but that the mark was held to be sufficient in that case. These cases were, in turn, cited as authoritative in the New York case of *Jackson* v. *Van Dusen* (1807) and later in the new Jersey Supreme Court case of *Den* v. *Mitton* (1830).[9] The chief justice noted in accordance with the Sussex Circuit Court opinion of 1827, where this latter case originated, that the choice of an illiterate marker as a witness may have been unwise, yet nonetheless permissable. The difficulties of illiteracy, particularly in cases of alleged fraud, having been thus recognized, the legitimacy of the mark was upheld:

> He who is unable to write his name, and makes his mark is, notwithstanding, a competent and legal witness to the execution of a will. It may be more difficult for him than for one who writes, after a lapse of time, to identify the instrument and to make the necessary proof; and in case of his absence or decease, it may be more difficult to obtain the requisite secondary proof, but the multiplication of difficulties, however imprudent the use of such a witness may be thereby rendered, or however commendable to select, where feasible, another person, does not amount to a legal disability or exclusion.[10]

The British case of *Cooper* v. *Bockett* (1844) offers an interesting contrast to the case of *Den* v. *Mitton* and illustrates well the influence of social class upon the testimony of an illiterate witness to a will. The document in question was one written by a Capt. Robert Spencer Cooper and witnessed by two of his servants, both of whom were illiterate. Two issues were at hand: (1) whether Cooper had signed the document previous to the witnessing and (2) whether changes had later been inserted into the will. The two illiterate witnesses, George and Mary Crittenden, had witnessed the will by tracing their signatures in pen over the penciled signatures done by Spencer for them. In dealing with the issue of the timing (order) of signatures, both Crittendens offered testimony. For our purposes the importance of the case lies in the arguments given to dispute the illiterates' testimony and the court's response to those arguments. In arguing for the Respondent Bockett, the attorneys attacked the legitimacy of the Crittendens' testimony by questioning their competency on the grounds of social class and illiteracy:

> Too much importance must not be given to the evidence of the attesting witnesses, who are illiterate persons; it would be dangerous to the interests of society, if witnesses of the class here subscribing were enabled to cut down a Will when called upon to depose to the exact order of circumstances attending the execution.[11]

The court's response noted with approval the line of arguments offered above. It stated that the evidence of the witnesses pertaining to the timing (order) of the signatures "ought to be received with caution and reserve." The court pointed to the contrast between the captain's social station and education and that of the servants. It was highly improbable, the court said, that a well-educated, well-informed man of the world would make a mistake in ordering of the signatures to a will. The evidence of the witnesses, on the other hand, was considered suspect because of their station in society, their probable degree of education, and lack of knowledge with respect to business dealings. In short, the court concluded that the memory of the witnesses was not to be trusted, and that in the absence of an issue of fraud, the probable intent of the educated person was to be trusted more than the testimony of lower class illiterates.[12]

Near the end of the nineteenth century the link presumed to exist between competency and illiteracy as indicated by the use of a mark is made explicit in the Georgia case of *Gillis* v. *Gillis* (1895):

> A witness who signs by his mark, if so capable of testifying, is just as competent a witness under the statute of frauds, our act of 1852 and section 2414 of the code, as one likewise capable of testifying who writes his own name.[13]

Thus, no inference as to the *in*competency of a witness to a document was to be made simply from the condition of being illiterate. Likewise, no inference about competency may be made either. The fact was simply that in the eyes of the law competency and witnessing a document by a mark were not related. The illiterate person was not presumed to be any less intelligent than the literate one. Fundamentally, it was a matter of priorities: the act of making one's last will and testament was of too great importance to be undermined by "eyesight, the continued sanity, the integrity, the memory, or the accessability of witnesses." The court in *Gillis* v. *Gillis* recognized that certain "evils" may stem from having illiterate or infirm persons, otherwise competent, attest to wills by their marks, but it did not deviate from the position that, other measures of competence aside, "all witnesses, learned and unlearned, vigorous or infirm," are placed "upon the same footing"; that illiteracy or infirmity will not count against them." [14]

The authority of the mark was firmly established throughout the nineteenth century in matters pertaining to the witnessing of documents, and the competency of witnesses was not necessarily suspect for their having been illiterate. It remains to look briefly at decisions involving illiterate witnessing under different circumstances. The few nineteenth-century cases involving illiterate witnesses in circumstances other than the signing of a will do not demonstrate a consistent pattern with respect to witness competency. Justices in these cases took note that some testimony of illiterate persons ought to be viewed with suspicion, but they were careful to avoid ruling out such testimony. In the Louisiana case of *Pillie* v. *Kenner* (1842), the court took the position that when an unimpeached witness is illiterate and "his statement extraordinary," it is admissible to substantiate it by demonstrating that the same statement was made at the time of the transaction.[15] In other words, the credibility of the illiterate witness is under some suspicion. The British case of *Johnston* v. *Todd* the following year is instructive by way of comparison. In this case the issue, insofar as it pertained to illiteracy, involved the veracity of an affidavit signed by an illiterate person. The court after referring to the general "infirmity of affidavit evidence" went on to comment specifically on illiterate witnesses:

> When the witness is illiterate and ignorant, the language presented to the Court is not his: it is, and must be, the language of the person who prepares the affidavit; and it may be, and too often is, the expression of that person's erroneous inference as to the meaning of the language used by the witness himself; and however carefully the affidavit may be read over to the witness, he may not understand what is said in language so different from that which he is accustomed to use. Having expressed his meaning in his own language, and finding it translated by a person on whom he relies into language not his own, and which he does not perfectly understand, he is too apt to acquiesce; and testimony not intended by him is brought before the Court as his.[16]

While the case was not tried before an American court, it clearly sets forth the dangers of witnessing by an illiterate person.

In the matter of witness competency, it is worth considering, also, *In the Matter of Cross* (1895). The case involved the appeal of Captain Cross, a New York City police officer who had been convicted of bribery, in part by the testimony of an illiterate witness. The bribe had been offered by the manager of a house of prostitution in New York City. The presiding justice observed that persons involved in business "who cannot read and write, have their faculty of memory more acutely educated, for the reason that they are compelled to depend upon their memory and cannot rely upon written memoranda."[17] The moral destitution of the manager of the "house" served finally to persuade the court that her testimony was not to be trusted, yet the analysis of her illiteracy and its bearing upon her memory is significant:

> The fact that this woman could not read and write, according to the common experience, tend to create in her a more accurate and retentive memory, because it would be upon her faculty that she must rely in the conduct of her affairs. Instead, therefore, of her incapacity to read and write accounting for her loss of memory, it seems to make it the more remarkable.[18]

Thus a theory of faculty psychology stressing the exercising of mental faculties provided the foundation for explaining why illiterates commonly were able to demonstrate superior recall skills. Strangely, the court used this assumption regarding the link between illiteracy and memory to discredit the witness's testimony. It concluded that "upon a consideration of the whole of her testimony that she was willfully forgetful and had not the slightest regard for the truthfulness of her testimony." [19] Although the profligacy of the witness persuaded the court to discount the testimony, it also made clear that illiteracy, far from being a detriment to the offering of proper testimony, could actually enhance its value.

Another dimension of the "marginality" of illiterate persons may be studied by examining cases dealing with juror qualifications. These decisions ordinarily involve the interpretation of statute law. In reviewing these, what one observes generally in the late nineteenth century is that marginality is differentiated by context, i.e., by the functional situation to which the illiterate juror must apply himself. At the same time it should be noted that different states varied in their statutory requirements for jurors, although a large number have some provision for literacy. Many states, as Proffatt observed in *A Treatise on Trial by Jury* (1880), required "a person to be well-informed and intelligent; and in some, it is further required that a person must be able to read and write the English language." In New York City, he notes, a person may not serve "unless he shall be an intelligent man of sound mind, and good character, free from legal exception, and able to read and write the English language understandingly." Even without such statutory provision, however, "it would be held," say, Proffatt, "that one ignorant of the language is not qualified." [20]

In dealing with illiteracy and juror competency, it is important to remember that justices of the courts were concerned with the function of the juror as it was affected by language skills in general. Thus, the ability to understand the language of the court was of first consideration. Oral literacy, if we may use the term, was of equal importance with visual literacy in interpreting evidence. From the court's viewpoint, functionality was the primary concern, and the adequacy of communications skills was interpreted according to the context of the case being heard. Many times this involved literacy in the traditional use of the term, but the problem of literacy was not exclusively a problem of print. It is unnecessary to pursue this latter point in any detail, since it lies outside the purview of traditional definitions of literacy. Two examples will suffice to make the point. In *The Lafayette Plankroad Co.* v. *The New Albany and Salem Railroad Co.* (1859), heard before the Indiana Supreme Court, the justices agreed with counsel for the appellants that a "competent juror must be a man of sound mind, of ordinary intelligence, and have a sufficient acquaintance with the English language to understand the evidence of the witnesses, and the instructions of the Court." [21] This included the ability to understand spoken English even though the juror may have been literate in another language. What was important was that the juror be functional within the context of legal proceedings; not to be so was to be materially illiterate. Again, in *Louisiana* v. *Push* (1871) it was held that "a person who only understands German, and does not understand English, is no more capable of sitting as a juror in the First District Court of New Orleans, where the proceedings are conducted entirely in English, than if he were deaf and dumb." [22]

Several cases in an eleven year period between 1867 and 1878 are helpful in illustrating the position of the courts with respect to level of education, literacy, and juror competency. The first of these was *The Commonwealth* v. *Winnermore,* a Pennsylvania case applied to the supreme court of the same state. A lower court had overruled the "challenge for cause of a juror," and this was upheld at the supreme court level. The juror was not classified as illiterate, but his low level of education raised essentially the same problems for the court. In giving its decision the high court noted that the ground for challenge of the juror "was want of education, rather than natural capacity or intelligence." The witness, observed the court, "could read but little; only read the newspapers; never read a book; and did not know his age." While this demonstrated a low level of education, said the court, "it did not show want of capacity to reason and judge of what was orally communicated." No statutory provision requiring a specified degree of learning as a prerequisite to be a juror existed in Pennsylvania, and "it does not follow that, because a man may not have read books, or may have confined his reading solely to the literature of the newspapers, he is not intelligent enough for a juryman." [23] Illiteracy, per se, was not a measure of juror competency in this case, although the court's dim view of reading only the newspaper reflects its own expectations of the educated man.

Several years later in the Mississippi case of *White* v. *The State* (1876) illiteracy was the point of contention. This case involved the murder of an infant child and was appealed, in part, on the grounds of juror incompetency. The court held that the inability to read and write was not a statutory disqualification of a juror for incompetency. "The law," said the court, "does not define an intellectual or educational standard." [24] In the same year in *Louisiana* v. *Louis* it was decided that "the law does not declare ignorance a disqualification in a juror which will authorize a party to challenge him for cause." [25] And again in 1878 in *American Life Insurance Company* v. *Mahone and Husband,* the Mississippi court held that juror qualifications as defined by statute did "not erect a standard of education or learning." [26]

These decisions which involved the question of educational level as related to juror competency were followed in the next two decades by a number of cases involving a juror's incompetency as determined by his inability to read and write English. Four of these were from Texas and Colorado; others were from Iowa, Mississippi, and Alabama. Two Texas cases demonstrate the critical importance of determining the competency of a juror on the basis of his literacy skills. In each the presence of an illiterate juror was material in determining the outcome of the case. In *Wright* v. *The State* (1882), adjudged in the Court of Appeals of the state of Texas, it was determined that the requirement for jurors to read and write employed in a Texas statute meant the ability to read and write English. The case, which was an appeal from a conviction for horse stealing, involved a challenge to a juror who possessed "a very fair knowledge of English," but who could only read and write German. In the court's opinion, the "defendant was deprived of a fair and impartial trial when there was forced upon him one juror who could not read and write the English language, and could not read the charge of the court for himself." [27] Thus the ability to simply understand English was not sufficient.

Four years later in *Johnson* v. *The State,* a case appealing a conviction for rape, the court concluded that one of the jurors was incompetent because his degree of literacy did not exceed his ability to write his name. Unlike most previous judicial decisions, the court in this case attempted to distinguish among levels of literacy and urged that a functional definition of literacy ought to be employed. The statute governing juror qualifications, said the court, "must have intended something practical":

> That a person can write his name certainly does not fill the measure of the statutory requirement that the juror should be able to *write.* We think that he should be able to express his ideas in words upon paper with pen or pencil.[28]

The import of the Florida case of *Jefferson County* v. *Lewis and Sons* (1884) was similar to that of *Johnson* v. *The State of Texas.* This former case centered around a suit brought by the defendants B. C. Lewis and Sons to recover damages upon bonds issued by Jefferson County. Among the various grounds of error upon which the appeal was made was that concerned with juror competency. In hearing the case in lower court, plaintiff's counsel had been permitted to examine the jurors "as to their ability to calculate interest, and to work interest in case of partial payments such as might arise upon the pleadings and proofs in this case." No error was committed in this procedure, observed the Florida Supreme Court, for the object "is to procure a jury sufficiently intelligent to understand the testimony and to render a proper verdict upon it." The statute cited was one of 1877 which provided "that when the nature of any case requires that a knowledge of reading, writing and arithmetic is necessary to enable a juror to understand the evidence to be offered on the trial, [then] it shall be a cause of challenge if he does not possess such qualification." In interpreting this statute, judges were given broad discretionary powers to determine whether the "practical education" of a juror was sufficient to handle "questions likely to arise on the trial." [29]

At a very basic level, the question of marginality is a question of who "belongs"; that is, it is a question of who is allowed to participate in the civic and economic life of a community. Thus the condition of being "marginal" rests upon the expectations of "significant others." To be marginal in a functional sense was often a product of the discretionary power of a judge. In general, the normative nature of the law requires that it be interpreted within a specific cultural context, and the link between juror competency and illiteracy is no exception. In many cases the illiterate person was specifically the target of statutory law, although the application of that law was left to justices of the courts. In dealing with the literacy requirements for juror competency the legal significance of literacy transcended the fortunes of the illiterates themselves; rather, it is clear that the lives and fortunes of others were at stake. Thus, illiteracy acquired a greater significance than if only the illiterate party were affected.

Contractual Relations and Illiteracy

In dealing with illiteracy and contract, it is important to note Pound's observation that "property and contract, security of acquisitions and security of transactions are the domain in which law is most effective and is chiefly invoked." [30] The scope of contractual relations is very broad, and the treatment here cannot pretend to be comprehensive. Some pivotal ideas in the history of English and American contract law, however, are worth reviewing.

The inviolability of contract is recognized by the United States Constitution, and the sanctity of contract along with its importance to social stability were ideas expressed often in the decisions of Chief Justice John Marshall. One of these *Ogden* v. *Saunders* (1827), a dissenting opinion and not as celebrated as cases like *Fletcher* v. *Peck, Dartmouth College* v. *Woodward,* or *Sturgis* v. *Crowninshield,* is nonetheless important for our purposes because it expresses the relationship of contractual obligations to natural rights theory. *Ogden* v. *Saunders* involved "the validity of a discharge in bankruptcy under a state statute enacted before the claim on which the suit was brought had come into existence." [31] Justices Marshall, Story, and Duvall dissented, arguing that whether prospective or retrospective, such bankruptcy laws ran counter to the Constitution's express language that "no State shall pass any law" "impairing the obligation of contracts." [32]

Marshall noted in his argument that the original power and right of individuals to contract was not derived from government, but, rather, brought with them into society. The right was "intrinsic," not derived from positive law, said Marshall, and resulted from "the right which every man retains to acquire property, to dispose of that property according to his own judgment, and to pledge himself for a future act." [33] The obligation of the contract "is a necessary consequence of the right to make it," noted Marshall. While the rights of contract are controlled by legislation, they are not given by it. Obligation and remedy in contractual matters are different, noted Marshall, and the language of the Constitution "is the language of restraint, not coercion"; it "prohibits the States from passing any law impairing the obligation of contracts [although] it does not enjoin them to enforce contracts." The sanctity of the obligation of contract thus lay in its being a natural right, and the obligation of contract derived

70

from "the act of the parties, not from the grant of government." Legislative provisions affecting the remedies for nonperformance, it was argued, ought not to be construed as affecting the obligation itself.[34]

The development of economic liberalism from the British utilitarians forward and the emergence of a natural rights theory of human behavior had exalted the idea of freedom of contract and free choice to a point where contractual relations were seen as the very foundation of civilized society. In the eighteenth century, Atiyah has noted, the "notion of contract, and the role of contract in society, were a great deal broader than they are today." Those who chose to speak to the issue perceived individual, private contractual relationships and the relationships of individuals to the state much in the same mold:

> . . . [men] chose to create a society in which free choice was one of their principal goals; they *voluntarily* created a society in which the voluntary creation of relationships would be permitted and respected; they *freely* instituted a society for the protection of their property in order that they could be free to acquire, exploit, or dispose of property to their best advantage.[35]

As the idea of free choice "swept all before it," observes Atiyah, "the paradigm of legal obligation came to be seen as that which was created by the deliberate and conscious choice of a man who made a promise; and by 1770 this was already beginning to lead to the conclusion that *all* legal obligations arose from free choice—which, if it was not expressed, must be implied." [36] It should not go unnoticed that this model for the "good" society, as it were, depended upon the educability of the public, for it had little chance to succeed in the absence of moral restraint and public enlightenment.

The increasing attention paid to the nature of contract in the eighteenth century did not necessarily mean that a full blown theory of modern contract law had emerged by this time. Horwitz has maintained that "modern contract law is fundamentally a creature of the nineteenth century" and that eighteenth-century contract law still carried with it the medieval tradition of substantive justice.[37] This, he argues, was true despite the wide acclaim given *Slade's Case* (1602) and the increasing importance of the action of debt. While executory contracts thus came at the end of the sixteenth century to imply that "when one agrees to pay money, or to deliver anything, he thereby assumes or promises to pay or deliver it," a "will" theory of contract did not emerge

71

until the nineteenth century.[38] Even in the eighteenth century, says Horwitz, contract law "was still dominated by a title theory of exchange, and damages were set under equitable doctrines that ultimately were to be rejected by modern contract law."[39] Thus Chancellor Desaussure of South Carolina (though not typical) argued as late as 1817 that

> It would be a great mischief to the community, and a reproach to the justice of the country, if contracts of very great inequality, obtained by fraud, or surprise, or the skillful management of intelligent men, from weakness, or inexperience, or necessity could not be examined into, and set aside.[40]

The *degree* to which Deaussure defended a theory of contract based upon equity was not typical, yet the concept of equity in contract still had defenders. Nathan Dean, who Horwitz identifies as one of the "most penetrating among the American treatise writers," argued in 1823 that "When an agreement appears very unequal, and affords any ground to suspect any imposition, unfairness, or undue power or command, the courts will seize any very slight circumstances to avoid enforcing it."[41] Thus an inequitable bargain was, in effect, evidence of a misrepresented bargain.

Pound has pointed out that following the decline of natural law theory, the historical theories of law in the nineteenth century, with the aid of metaphysical jurists, helped to make individual free will "the central point in the theory of law."[42] The emergence of a modern "will" theory of contract in which contractual obligations depend upon the "convergence of individual desires" reflected important shifts in attitude when dealing with property. Modern contract law in the nineteenth century accompanied the growth of extensive markets where goods "came to be thought of as fungible; the function of contracts correspondingly shifted from that of simply transferring title to a specific item to that of ensuring an expected return."[43] We are speaking of executory contracts here, and in a very real and sometimes painful sense we should note that courts had come to recognize the commercial interests of urban America. This had become clear in the "absorption of commodities transactions under contract law"[44] and is evident in the increased acceptance of the doctrine of caveat emptor. Fraud and misrepresentation were not to be allowed, it is true, but these were narrowly construed. Says Atiyah, "Prima facie a man must rely on his own judgment, and not on what the other party says in the normal process of negotiation."[45] Even in his attack on caveat emptor, Gulian Verplanck, legal theorist and author of *An Essay on the Doctrine of Contracts* (1825), noted that "full knowledge of all material facts" was all the law could oversee, and these did not include "peculiar advantages of skill, shrewdness, and experience, regarding which . . . no one has a right to call upon us to abandon." [46] In short, the latitude for negotiating inequitable executory contracts (and quasi-executory contracts) had considerably broadened by the nineteenth century. The question which I wish to consider, then, is the extent to which the illiterate person was affected by the rise of freedom of contract in general and the extent to which his marginality was increased because his illiteracy did not allow him to express his will.

"No contract can exist, unless there be a mutual consent of the parties, and an intelligent understanding of its terms," said William Story in 1844.[47] This general rule applied to both illiterates and literates, since there is no doubt that "natural incapacity" was not associated with illiteracy, and, as we have seen, there was no assumption that the intelligence of the illiterate person was any lower than that of the literate individual. In nineteenth-century cases involving illiteracy and contract, the courts were acutely aware of the difficulties of the illiterate person when entering into contract, the basis for which was mutual consent and the "convergence of individual desires." In *Atwood* v. *Cobb* (1834) the validity of an executory contract for the sale of land was in question partly because the intention of the illiterate party to the contract were difficult to determine. The case illustrates clearly the concern of the court with the problem of illiteracy. In delivering the opinion of the court, Chief Justice Shaw noted that "the intent of the parties, if possible, is to be ascertained, without regard to technical rules":

> . . . considering how often agreements are necessarily drawn up by illiterate persons, incapable of expressing their intentions with clearness and certainty, and the injurious consequences which would follow if affect should be given to such agreements, it must be a rule of construction governing courts of justice, not wholly to reject such instruments, as uncertain, if it is possible, with the helps allowed to be brought to the aid of such construction, to ascertain the meaning of the parties.[48]

Shaw had surely pointed to the most difficult of the problems in dealing with illiterate parties to a contract: the intent of their actions. For this reason decisions by courts were often "compensatory" in nature, not in the sense that they attempted to judge the equity of contracts, but in the sense that they consistently safeguarded the rights of illiterate persons against fraud and misrepresentation occurring as a result of the inability to read. In this stand they were adhering to Blackstonian principles governing the reading of a deed, which, it should be remembered, were extended to all written documents. The case of *Rogers* v. *Place* (1867) in Indiana noted specifically that the rule according to Blackstone is that wherever any party desires it, the deed must be read to him, and:

> If he can, he should read it himself; if he be blind or illiterate, another must read it to him. If it be read falsely, it will be void; at least for so much as is mis-recited.[49]

A number of cases could be documented to demonstrate the difficulties facing illiterate parties to a contract in the nineteenth century. The following three, however, are illustrative. The first (1870) involved the defense of a fraud case, the plaintiff being Mr. Atchison, a man who was unable to read and write and who had signed a note for $140. In 1868 two men had gone to the home of Atchison proposing that he become an agent to sell reapers, screw-forks, and mowers. At first he declined to do this on the ground that he would not become bound for anything. The strangers assured him he would incur no obligation, and he then assented. The implements were to be sent to him and sold on commission, the terms being agreed upon. The two men then proposed to give him an instrument for Atchison's protection in making sales since the articles had been patented. The document was presented to Atchison for his signature, and, since he was unable to read it without difficulty, he requested that it be read to him. One of the men then purposefully "misread" the document. They then produced another paper, which they assured Atchison was a duplicate of the one read to him, and he signed both papers. The papers were much larger in size than an ordinary note, and Atchison was unaware that he had signed a note. The papers, as it turned out, were merely a ruse to obtain Atchison's signature on a $140 note. Fortunately for Atchison, his credibility was greater than that of the opportunists, and the litigation was settled in his favor.[50]

The second case, *Walker* v. *Ebert* (1870), involved Mr. Ebert, a German by birth and education who was unable to read and write the English language. Ebert alleged that the holders of a note bearing his signature had cheated him by falsely claiming that he would become the sole agent for his town of a certain patented machine for a period of ten years. One of the machines was to be delivered to him free of cost, excluding freight, and Mr. Ebert was to receive 50 percent of all profits from his sales. The holders then presented to him a sign, in duplicate, an instrument partly written and partly printed which he was unable to read and which was stated to be simply a contract covering the oral agreement. The original decision in favor of Walker was reversed and a new trial ordered.[51]

Finally, the case of *Trambly* v. *Ricard et al.* (1880) involved what was probably a common occurrence in settling a home: the purchase of furniture. The plaintiff in this instance had purchased furniture on credit and contended that, by oral agreement, he had agreed upon a price, part of which was paid down, the rest to be paid by installments. The agreement was then committed to writing. The plaintiff testified that the written agreement was not that agreed upon orally and that the written agreement had been obtained by fraud; nothing, said the plaintiff, had been said of borrowing or renting the furniture. Later, when the defendants came to remove the furniture from the premises, suit was brought for trespass to real estate. In delivering the opinion of the court (which had only to decide whether or not a jury might find fraud in this case), it was noted that the illiteracy of the plaintiff was of "controlling importance," and the literate party was "bound to show that he [the illiterate party] fully understood the object and import of the writings sought to be enforced against him":

> A party who is ignorant of the contents of a written instrument, from inability to read, who signs it without intending to, and who is chargeable with no negligence in not ascertaining the character of it, is no more bound than if it were a forgery.[52]

Prior to the late 1890s cases involving disputed contracts noted that a *literate* person who signs a written instrument without reading it or having it read has no legal recourse on grounds of ignorance of the contract. In the absence of fraud or misrepresentation the literate individual is assumed to exercise his ability to read and "the law affords no relief." [53] Illiterate parties to a contract, on the other hand, were to receive some special consideration for their disability. In fact, the burden for specifying the intent of the contract and conveying that intent to an illiterate party was clearly with the literate person. A number of decisions clearly demonstrate this point, but two will suffice for illustration.

The first of these cases, *Seldon* v. *Myers* (1857), was heard before the Supreme Court of the United States, and involved a dispute over property in Washington, D.C., owned by Seldon, a restaurant owner. Seldon had deeded his property to Lawrence Myers and Company of New York, the suppliers of liquor to his restaurant. In addition, Seldon had signed a promissory note in order to have credit extended to him. Seldon was an illiterate and claimed that it was his understanding that only a portion of the property had been deeded. The testimony of Myers claimed that all the property had been deeded and that the contract (deed) had been read to Seldon explaining "its object, the amount of the note, . . . the description of the property and the purposes." The Court held in favor of Myers and Company on the grounds that no fraud had been committed and there was no conclusive evidence to demonstrate that the deed had been incorrectly read and explained to Seldon. In delivering the decision, it was noted that in dealing with an unlettered man "it is incumbent on Myers and Company to show, past doubt, that he [Seldon] fully understood the object and import of the writings upon which they are proceeding to charge him." It was observed by the Court that had the Company failed to give a correct reading to the illiterate party, it "would have furnished strong grounds for inferring that he had been deceived, and had not understood the meaning of the written instruments he signed." [54]

A second case illustrates the same principle and was heard in the New Jersey Court of Chancery. The case of *Suffern and Galloway* v. *Butler and Butler* (1867) involved a dispute over terms to lease mineral rights. The defendants (Butler and Butler) in this case were illiterate and alleged that the lease had been improperly read to them: "he purposely omitted it [the disputed clause] and if it had been read, they never would have signed the same." [55] In deciding the case, the chancellor observed that the defendant offered a "positive denial" that the lease had been read properly:

> He cannot read, and in his case the reading of the lease correctly is as material to the execution of it as making his mark. [56]

It is important to realize, also, that in cases of illiterate contracting parties the courts do not presume any particular level of intelligence for the illiterate persons. As long as the contract was "honestly and fairly read or explained," said the court in *Green* v. *Maloney* (1894), it is not necessary "to show that the illiterate did understand its contents and their nature." "If, after a paper has been read or explained to him," observed the court, "he sign it, making no objection to it, nor request any explanation of it, he must, in all reason be taken to have known what he was signing." [57]

The responsibility of the literate party to accurately portray the contents of a contract with an illiterate person is a principle that has remained in force in the twentieth century. When, however, the illiteracy of one of the contracting parties is not evident and the literate party does not realize that he is dealing with an illiterate person, the situation is substantially different. Thus, in the 1931 case of *Sharpless-Hendler Ice Cream Co.* v. *Davis,* the court noted that "the fact of illiteracy is of no materiality and . . . the contract is binding" when an illiterate person, "unknown to the other party to be illiterate, chose to affix her name to an agreement without demanding that it be read to her, and without being misled . . . by the other party." The court continued: "He is bound, if he did not require the document to be read to him." [58] This latter principle was laid down in Thoroughgood's case in the late sixteenth century and had been reiterated in Story's *Commentaries on Equity Jurisprudence.* Yet, between 1850 and 1898, contract cases involving this principle are few, while cases citing the responsibility of the literate party are plentiful. Following Belliwith's case (1898), however, there are frequent occasions in which the responsibility of the illiterate person looms large. Thus, with the coming of the twentieth century, a subtle shift in emphasis is apparent, a shift which certainly placed greater responsibility on the illiterate to look out for his own welfare.

In the case of *Chicago, St. P., M. and O. Ry.* v. *Belliwith* (1898), Belliwith, an illiterate German peddler who understood English, had been injured by an explosion as a result of attempting to retrieve a package which he had left on a train, said train having been stopped as a result of another train wreck. In the process, Belliwith had been burned and subsequently filed suit against the railway company for negligence. Belliwith had been awarded a modest amount in damages and had signed a release for liability on the part of the railway. Following this agreement, however, Belliwith instituted suit against the company, claiming that he had not understood the terms of the release because of his illiteracy. In delivering his opinion, Sanborn opened his remarks by explaining the sanctity of a written contract:

A written contract is the highest evidence of the terms of an agreement between the parties to it, and it is the duty of every contracting party to learn and know its contents before he signs and delivers it. He owes this duty to the other party to the contract because the latter may, and probably will, pay his money and shape his action in reliance upon the agreement. He owes it to the public, which, as a matter of public policy, treats the written contract as a conclusive answer to the question, what was the agreement? [59]

The court noted that if Belliwith had not asked that the contract (release) be read to him, this constituted "gross negligence" on his part; if the contract had indeed been read to him as his attorney testified, then he had signed it in full cognizance of its terms and thus acceded to them:

> He was willing to receive, and did receive, the $300 for this release, without reading it or hearing it read; and he cannot be, and ought not to be, now heard, while he retains its benefits, to say that his own ignorance and negligence exempt him from its obligations.[60]

The principle of negligent ignorance is frequently cited in cases following *Belliwith*. A number of these cases involved initial oral agreements which had preceded written documents, the latter sometimes having been altered from the original agreement. While misrepresentation was present in some cases, the principle of negligent ignorance was often cited as in the Alabama case of *Bates* v. *Harte* (1901):

> One who has signed a contract in negligent ignorance of its contents cannot, in the absence of fraud and misrepresentation, set up such ignorance in avoidance of the obligation. If he cannot read, due care for his own interest requires that he should have it read to him.[61]

And again in *Shores-Mueller Co.* v. *Lonning* (1913), it was noted that "one who signs a contract is bound to exercise reasonable care and prudence to inform himself as to its contents . . .": ". . . if he does not read or have it read, the law will presume that he did his duty [and] will not permit him to say that he did not read [it]." [62] What was to be preserved, noted J. Mason in *Burns* v. *Spiker* (1921), was the "value of all contracts." [63] The written contract was assumed to be the final agreement reached by contracting parties and "to merge all prior negotiations." [64] In short, what was at stake in the issue of illiteracy and contract was the sanctity of the contract, in fact, the social edifice built upon contract.

Conclusion

The functional relationship of the illiterate person to the judicial system has been of paramount importance in the consideration of the civic, social, and economic meanings of literacy in nineteenth-century America. While the findings may be considered tentative and await further study, several of them should be restated. First, it is evident that many illiterate persons were not relegated to a "marginal" position simply by virtue of their having been illiterate. The marker, dependent as he was upon others for expressing his intent, nonetheless did not find his position a demeaning one. The authority and legitimacy of the mark was preserved despite the attendant difficulties of fraud recognized by the courts in their repeated warnings about the use of illiterate witnesses for documents. Nor did illiteracy infer a lack of intelligence, although courts viewed the testimony of some illiterates with suspicion. Rather, it was the general position of the courts that illiteracy was a disability akin to blindness, but not debilitating in terms of native capacity to understand.

Juror competency raised a more difficult question for the courts than did the witnessing of documents. Clearly, a competent juror ought to understand the proceedings of the court and, in certain instances, be able to read pertinent documents. Perhaps because the social and civil significance of the juror's judgment was broader than that of witnessing a single document, courts were more stringent in allowing illiterates to function in this role. In general, no intellectual or educational standard, per se, was set for juror competency, yet the criterion of functionality demanded certain levels of communication skills. *Level* of literacy was important, and, as we have seen, the simple ability to write one's name was considered insufficient in *Johnson* v. *The State* (1886).

Finally, in the matter of contracts, nineteenth-century justices consistently demonstrated an awareness of problems occasioned by one or more of the contracting parties being illiterate. Yet, at the same time, courts were faced with the problem of guaranteeing the rights of all parties. A meeting of the minds, of wills, of intent was of first importance in a contractual agreement, yet intent was difficult to determine for the illiterate person. The general rule of parol evidence had made oral agreements unenforceable when followed by a written contract. The illiterate person, then, relied upon the words of others—in many cases, persons with whom he was unfamiliar, who were not part of a local community, and with whom the first contact would be the last.

Protection for the illiterate party to a contract became increasingly difficult within the context of an ideal free market economy which demanded that the individuals be left alone to contract freely, yet insisted, in the name of sanctity of contract, that economic and social stability be preserved. Order and freedom competed for the loyalties of justices; individual discretion in the use of one's resources was to be balanced against the need for regulation.[65] During most of the nineteenth century, courts seemed to make an effort to preserve the rights of illiterate contracting parties and to protect these persons against abuses stemming from the inability to read and write. By the end of the nineteenth century, however, the emphasis had shifted. While both a literate and an illiterate party were obligated to express accurately the contents of an agreement, no longer did the major responsibility seem to lie with the literate person. Rather, it had become clear that the illiterate person was bound to inform himself and to take the initiative in securing a correct reading of the contract. Where the concept of contract was presumed to be the foundation of social order itself, freedom of contract demanded individual responsibility from all parties.

Notes

1. George L. Haskins, "Law and Colonial Society," *American Quarterly* 9 (1957): 43.

2. James Willard Hurst, "Legal Elements in United States History," in Donald Fleming and Bernard Bailyn, eds., *Law in American History* (Boston: Little, Brown and Co., 1971).

3. 259 N.C. 359.

4. The concept of marginality is closely tied to the presumption that illiteracy is a form of isolation and that the "illiterate is unable to communicate with his fellows in written symbols and hence is largely restricted to immediate social groups for many forms of social stimuli." (UNESCO, *The Experimental World Literacy Programme: A Critical Assessment* [UNPO, 1976], p. 118.) Graff has summed up the prevailing view of the illiterate as a marginal person by noting that:

Their dire position leaves the illiterates outside the dominant social processes . . . exacerbating their own disadvantages and enlarging the loss they represent to the society and the economy . . . . Moreover, their existence threatens the function of internalized

controls and the successful operation of a democratic participatory social order. (Harvey J. Graff, *The Literacy Myth, Literacy and Social Structure in the Nineteenth Century City* [New York: Academic Press, 1979], pp. 53–54).

5. Horwitz observes that "modern contract law is fundamentally a creature of the nineteenth century." A theory of equity dominated eighteenth-century contract and, as he notes, "the most important aspect of the eighteenth-century conception of exchange is an equitable limitation on contractual obligation." "Under the modern will theory," he continues, "the extent of contractual obligation depends upon the convergence of individual desires. The equitable theory, by contrast, limited and sometimes denied contractual obligations by reference to the fairness of the underlying exchange." (Morton J. Horwitz, "The Historical Foundations of Modern Contract Law," *Harvard Law Review* 87 (1974): 919, 923; reprint in Wythe Holt, ed., *Essays in Nineteenth-Century American Legal History* (Westport, Conn.: Greenwood Press, 1976), pp. 206, 210. A similar point is made by P. S. Atiyah for Great Britain

in *The Rise and Fall of Freedom of Contract* (Oxford: Clarendon Press, 1979). The shift from an equity to a will theory of contract has been most important in matters dealing with commerce and business activity where future agreements are at stake. The will theory of contract is evident in other contractual relations as well, however, and is useful for conceptualizing problems of the illiterate in communicating his intent.

6. *Thoroughgood* v. *Cole*, 2 Eng. Rep. 9; Shulter's Case, 12 Eng. Rep., 90; Sir William Blackstone, *Commentaries on the Laws of England in Four Books*, ed. William Draper Lewis (Philadelphia: Rees Welsh and Co., 1900), 2:304–5.

7. *Thoroughgood* v. *Cole*, 2 Eng. Rep. at 9.

8. Lee Soltow and Edward Stevens, *The Rise of Mass Literacy and the Common School in the United States: A Socio-Economic Analysis to 1870.* (Chicago: The University of Chicago Press, 1981), p. 46.

9. *Harrison* v. *Harrison*, 8 Vez. 185; *Den v. Mitton*, 7 N.J.L. 70. In *Horton* v. *Johnson*, Justice Lumpkin of the Supreme Court of Georgia delivered the opinion that "while the name of the *testator* may be signed by a third person, provided it be done in his presence and by his express directions, no such indulgence is extended to the subscription by the witness." (*Horton* v. *Alexander*, Ga. 396 [1855]).

10. *Den* v. *Mitton*, 7 N.J.L. at 73.

11. 13 Eng. Rep. 369.

12. Ibid., 372–73.

13. 96 Ga. 5.

14. Id. at 6–13.

15. 2 Rob. 96.

16. 49 Eng. Rep. 711.

17. 92 Hun. 355.

18. Id. at 355–56.

19. Id. 356.

20. John Profatt, *A Treatise on Trial by Jury* (San Francisco: Summer Whitney and Co., 1880), pp. 164–65.

21. 13 Ind. 101.

22. 23 La. Ann. 14. Two later cases prove an exception to the general rule and illustrate well the bending of the court to practical considerations. Both are Colorado cases and should be seen in light of the cultural pluralism of that state with its large number of Mexican-American residents unequally distributed among the various counties of the state. These basic social and demographic facts were significant factors in determining juror competency and its relation to literacy. In *The Town of Trinidad* v. *Simpson* (1879), the major issue at stake was one of juror competency. The court was, in effect, asked to interpret a Colorado statute covering juror qualifications—a statute, however, which did not refer to the subject of literacy. Thus the grounds for challenging juror competency stood on common law principles rather than statute law, and it behooved the justices of the court to consider the matter historically. In reviewing the arguments of Sir Edward Coke and Blackstone, it was observed that a "defect in education" which renders a juror unable to understand court proceedings conducted in a language other than the juror's vernacular clearly makes it impossible for the juror to discharge his duties. When no aid (such as an interpreter) is forthcoming, "ignorance of the language . . . is as conspicuously a disqualifying circumstance as though he were deaf." The statute under George II, remembered the court, had been carried forward to the people of Colorado and the United States, and it should be assumed, said the court, that in the silence of the statute "all judicial proceedings would be conducted in English." It did not follow, however, that this would be "exclusively so," since non-English speaking witnesses could testify with the aid of an interpreter and contracts

written in a "foreign tongue" could be dealt with. Thus, concluded the court, instructions of the court to jurors might be translated into Spanish "for the use and instruction of a juror understanding that language alone" (5 Colo. 66–70). Ten years later this decision was reaffirmed in *In re Allison* (1889), and the court, noting the practicalities of administering justice, observed:

> In certain counties of the state where the great bulk of the population originally were, and a very large proportion thereof still are, Mexicans, it would, for many years, have been practically impossible to have administered justice, under our system of jurisprudence, without their aid in this capacity. (13 Colo. 525)

23. 2 Brew. 380.

24. 52 Miss. 224.

25. 28 La. Ann. 84.

26. 56 Miss. 194.

27. 12 Texas Ct. App. 164, 168.

28. 21 Texas Ct. App. 379.

29. 20 Fla. 998.

30. Roscoe Pound, *An Introduction to the Philosophy of Law* (New Haven: Yale University Press, 1922), p. 193.

31. Joseph P. Cotton, ed., *The Constitutional Decisions of John Marshall,* 2 Vols. (New York: G. P. Putnam's Sons, 1905), 2:175.

32. *Ogden* v. *Saunders* (1827) in Cotton, *The Constitutional Decisions of John Marshall,* 2:180.

33. Id. at 198.

34. Id. at 205, 209.

35. Atiyah, *The Rise and Fall of Freedom of Contract,* p. 36.

36. Id. at 57.

37. Morton J. Horwitz, "Foundations of Modern Contract Law," p. 204.

38. See also Frederick G. Kempin, Jr., *Legal History, Law and Social Change*

(New York: Prentice-Hall Inc., 1963), p. 83.

39. Horwitz, "Historical Foundations of Modern Contract Law," p. 207.

40. Id. at 210. In the matter of equity, notes Barbour, the chancellor "exercised a wide jurisdiction over contract in the fifteenth century where there was no remedy at law." This is especially evident in "petitions brought against vendors for non-performance of contracts to convey land." These actions, it should be remembered, always involved agreements by parol and were often informal. This informality of the agreements made them unenforceable at common law. If there were a deed, the common law provided action in covenant. (W. T. Barbour, "The History of Contract in Early English Equity," in *Oxford Studies in Social and Legal History,* ed. P. Vinogradoff (Oxford: Clarendon Press, 1914), pp. 116–18. The place of the concept of equity is discussed in Stanley N. Katz, "The Politics of Law in Colonial America: Controversies over Chancery Courts in Equity Law in the Eighteenth Century," in Donald Fleming and Bernard Bailyn, eds., *Law in American History* (Boston: Little, Brown and Co., 1971). Katz notes that proceedings of equity in chancery were designed to remedy defects in common law as a result of its inflexibility. The chancellor, says Katz, operated on the Aristotelian principle "that the essence of equity is the correction of positive law where that fails because too generally formulated." "Equity," he continues, "was thus an attempt to make law supple enough to do substantial justice throughout the broad range of human experience accessible to the power of the state" (Katz 259).

41. Horwitz, 237.

42. Roscoe Pound, *The Formative Era of American Law* (Boston: Little, Brown and Co., 1938), p. 114.

43. Id. at 205.

44. Id. at 228.

45. Atiyah, 403.

46. Horwitz, 236.

47. William W. Story, *A Treatise on the Law of Contracts not under Seal* (Boston: Charles C. Little and James Brown, 1844), p. 13.

48. 15 Mass. 229.

49. 29 Ind. 582.

50. *Taylor* v. *Atchison* 54 Ill. 196 (1870).

51. 29 Wis. 194.

52. 130 Mass. 259.

53. *Seeright* v. *Fletcher* 6 Blackf. 381 (1843); *May* v. *Johnson and Another* 3 Ind. 449 (1852); *Rogers* v. *Place* 29 Ind. 580 (1868).

54. 20 U.S. 509–511 (1857).

55. Id.

56. 18 N.J. Eq., 222.

57. 8 Del. 26.

58. 15 A. 248.

59. 83 F. 439.

60. Id. at 440.

61. 124 Ala. 431.

62. 140 S. W. 199; see also *Erickson* v. *Knights of the Maccabees of the World* 203 Pac. 674 (1922) and *Standard Motor Company* v. *Samuel Peltzer* 147 Md. 509 (1925).

63. 202 Pac. 371.

64. *Autin* v. *Brooklyn Cooperage Co.* 285 S. W. 1017 (1926).

65. James Willard Hurst, *Law and the Conditions of Freedom in Nineteenth-Century United States* (Madison: University of Wisconsin Press, 1956), pp. 5–14.

Functional Literacy in
Nineteenth-Century China

by Evelyn S. Rawski

Evelyn Rawski, professor of history at the University of Pittsburgh, has re-searched a broad range of topics in the history of China during the last four centuries and is the author of a number of books and papers that present the results of those investigations. In Education and Popular Literacy in Ch'ing China *(Ann Arbor: University of Michigan Press, 1979), she deals with the movement for popular literacy before the 1911 revolution.*

Drawing on her work on education and popular culture, Professor Rawski argues for recognition of the relatively high degree of literacy achieved in China by the end of the last century. The success of that literacy experiment is traced to the support provided by the culture, the expectation of rewards for learning, and the usefulness of what was taught.

In a nonalphabetic language such as Chinese, literacy cannot be acquired through the memorization of a small number of symbols, but demands knowledge of many distinct characters for reading and writing. The Chinese had no phonetic syllabary, as did the Japanese, to ease the task, nor was there any concept of limited or functional literacy in traditional China. Those who were considered educated had mastered the orthodox classical curriculum, which was dominated by the Confucian classics and the large corpus of scholarly commentaries, histories, and literary materials handed down from previous centuries. This curriculum was well-defined and universal through the empire and was in-tended to prepare students for the civil service examinations and thence for government service. Advanced literacy was the virtual monopoly of a very small group of men who formed the elite of the society.

Of course, many Chinese were able to read at lower levels of skill, even though they were not considered educated by the standards of their culture. Because they possessed knowledge of only a limited number of characters, such persons usually had narrowly specialized vocabularies. As one missionary noted, "Multitudes can read the characters so as to know the names of hundreds of them without being able to read a book," yet at the same time, "know the characters they require in their business; it may be a hundred or a thousand. They can often read and write business letters, but they cannot read even a single book at sight." [1]

The practical value of such specialized vocabularies has been confirmed by twentieth-century mass education movements which have aimed at teaching from several hundred up to fifteen hundred characters to adult illiterates. Educators involved with these efforts began to analyze various kinds of written materials in order to identify the most frequently used characters that should be given priority in teaching. In one study of character frequency, it was found that a person who could recognize 9 characters could read 1 out of 7 characters in simple material, while knowledge of 78 characters enabled him to read 50 percent, 352 characters to read 70 percent, and 1169 characters to read 91 percent of the same material. The mass education movement concluded that knowledge of twelve hundred characters gave a total vocabulary of "well over 2,000 words." [2] Separate readers teaching twelve hundred basic characters were developed for urban residents, farmers, and soldiers: completion of the readers allowed graduates to read simple books, write letters, and keep accounts. The course, to be completed in six weeks, furnished Chinese with functional literacy.

In traditional China, literacy was largely though not wholly confined to men. Formal education for women was not sanctioned by Chinese society. Even educated men often held the view that ignorance was a virtue in women, although literate women were also most likely to be found in such well-to-do households. We learn about these literate women through chance references in writings about and by their male kin as the mothers, sisters, and aunts who guided children through their first lessons within the home. These women enjoyed access to education through their literate male relatives. Once educated, their ability to keep accounts and household records undoubtedly helped them fulfill their domestic duties. Special textbooks for women like the *Female's Classic of Filial Piety* (Nü hsiao-ching) or *Female's Analects* (Nü lun-yü) existed, suggesting a fair degree of female literacy in elite households. Among villagers, female literacy was much rarer. For households who had difficulty financing the education of a son, educating a girl was like "weeding the field of some other man." [3] A son was a permanent member of the Chinese partilineal family, but a daughter was a transient, someone who would marry and belong thereafter to her husband's family. The education of daughters was viewed as a waste of scarce resources by her natal family. Despite some regional exceptions, only 1 to 10 percent of women in the nineteenth century were literate.[4]

Reports of male literacy come to us from Westerners who lived in the treaty ports. Foreign residents in the 1830s observed, "Of the whole population of Canton, not more than one half are able to read. Perhaps not 1 boy out of 10 is left entirely destitute of instruction; yet of the other sex not 1 in 10 ever learns to read and write." [5] Others wrote about the plentitude of books in China and remarked on the circulating libraries renting books to the servants and coolies working in Western establishments. They even found books modeled after Chinese reading primers that were designed to teach Portuguese and English phonetically, selling for "a penny or two" to servants, coolies, and shopkeepers.

But Canton was a highly atypical city in the nineteenth century, the center of one of the most densely populated regions of China, the Pearl River delta. Its inhabitants were unusually literate. How do we determine the general literacy rates for nineteenth-century China, given the absence of overall statistics? In a recent study, I have culled various estimates of literacy for the nineteenth and twentieth centuries, gathered information on the distribution of private and other schools, on the supply of potential teachers, and examined the cost of schooling to arrive at the conclusion that from 30 to 45 percent of Chinese males attended school in the late nineteenth century and possessed functional literacy skills.[6]

Cultural Context

What was the cultural environment that made this level of literacy possible? There was and is a "profound reverence" for schooling among Chinese, due first to the universal recognition that education was the key to prestige, power, and wealth in late imperial China, because it alone provided entry to bureaucratic careers. The Ch'ing dynasty (1644–1911) continued the trend toward limiting entry to the civil service outside the examinations, so that ambitious young men had to study in order to compete for the examination degrees that qualified them to hold office. Government service, the most honorable calling in the original Confucian order, brought with it political power and personal reward, so the motivation for education was high.

By the nineteenth century the civil service examinations were open to all males but a very small minority. There was a fully articulated hierarchy of examinations, beginning at the county level and moving, at the very end, to the palace in Peking itself. The highest degrees, won at the provincial and national competitions, qualified their holders for office. Regulations and institutional arrangements sought to insure the impersonality of the grading. A fairly fixed quota system combined with population growth during the eighteenth and early nineteenth centuries to add to the keenness of the competition.[7] But the potential rewards were so great that families were willing to invest large sums of money in education, sums that were large not only in an absolute sense but as a percentage of the total family assets. This was because an individual's success in the examinations ensured the success of his whole family. Since only a very few were able to win degrees, families tried to select their brightest sons for the prolonged education necessary to prepare for the examinations, but talent first had to be identified, and that meant exposing a much larger number of boys to the first phases of schooling. The lure of examination success thus led families to send boys to school who might then drop out after a few years when their lack of ability became evident.

The case of Chu Te, the famous Red Army leader, illustrates this point. Chu, born in 1886 in Szechwan province, was one of three sons in a family of tenant farmers who were "too poor to eat rice except on rare occasions." Yet Chu and his two older brothers were sent to a private school, which charged 800 cash as tuition for the eldest and 200 cash each for the two younger boys. This poor tenant family, straining every resource, was able to pay these sums. When Chu Te and one brother continued their lessons at a better school run by the wealthy landlord and boasting a teacher with a lower academic degree, the same fees were charged. Chu's family used its savings to educate its sons; of the three brothers, one dropped out after a year, the second after three years, while Chu Te was allowed to go on for further schooling.[8]

The prestige accorded to education percolated down to the villages, where a peasant who sent his sons to school thereby gained "face" and raised his status in the community. But there were also considerable rewards for literacy in everyday life. Since the government tried to regulate trade, there were innumerable official notices, regulations, and documents for merchants and shopkeepers to read, fill, and file in addition to their own accountbooks. Enterprises as lowly in status as the porter's trade, said to be staffed with landless men from the villages, required tickets and schedules of carrying charges. Written contracts were ubiquitous, to be used for purchasing or mortgaging real estate, for renting land, hiring laborers, borrowing money, and even for selling children.[9]

Advances in China's economy were reflected in many villages, where a "sizable fraction" of persons were "engaged in occupations clearly not those of peasants." The extensive participation of villagers in marketing and the importance of written materials in their relations with government made literacy a valuable asset. The government systems of police security and tax collection, the *pao-chia* and *li-chia*, required that written records be kept and shifted about by householders. The Ch'ing government used written notices to transmit regulations to its rural as well as urban populace; we know of attempts to put such communications in simple language and "nice calligraphy, easy to read" for the benefit of those who were not fully literate.[10]

Many farmers in north as well as central and south China participated in water control organizations. Since irrigation systems often encompassed several villages, the coordination of work and allocation of water were quite complicated tasks. Records had to be kept of the schedule for drawing water, for assessing households for labor and funds to keep up the dikes and irrigation ditches. These organizations rotated the supervisory and recordkeeping duties among landowning farmers, who must thus have been functionally literate.

Literacy was essential "not only for scholarship and official administration, but for successful farm management and commerce, and it was extremely useful if not essential for those wishing to assume a greater than ordinary influence in the local affairs of their neighborhood or village."[11] Families used literacy as a defense against being cheated. P. T. Ho cites a family of agricultural tenants in east China, bilked by a villager over a land deal, who sent a son through school, "for without an educated man, the family could not defend itself against local sharpers in the future."[12] Ch'ing society thus provided positive incentives for schooling for farmers as well as urban tradesmen and the elite.

In comparison with other premodern societies, China also had an unusually large pool of potential teachers, more than enough to teach the 30 to 45 percent of the male population who are estimated to have attended school. Most frequently teachers were men with lower examination degrees who were fully literate but not qualified to hold government posts. School regulations identify holders of the *t'ung-sheng* and *sheng-yuan* degrees, obtained by passing examinations at the county and prefectural levels, as potential teachers for beginning students. As this group numbered 2.9 million in 1850, there was a maximum of six potential teachers per thousand people. If we compare the supply of potential teachers with the estimated number of school-age boys in 1850, we find that it was theoretically possible to teach every male child with a class size of only sixteen, so it was certainly possible to educate the smaller group of boys attending school.[13]

And there were definite incentives for scholars to support themselves by teaching while attempting to win higher degrees: teaching was a very respectable occupation, for had not Confucius himself been a teacher? By contrast, anecdotes and government prohibitions indicate that in the struggle to keep themselves alive, scholars of modest means had ignored statutory restrictions against engaging in such "degrading" occupations as store bookkeeper, clerk, local broker, and government runner (a low status, unpaid post in government offices). Indigent degree-holders might earn a living by fortune-telling, which in its more prestigious forms, like geomancy, was respected as a highly developed science. After all, they could sink much lower; it was not only in novels that scholars were reduced to collecting night soil for a living. Feng Yün-shan, a leader of the Taiping rebellion that tore through China in the mid-nineteenth century, was a lower degree-holder who was forced at one time to work gathering the harvest, carrying earth and collecting pig and buffalo manure for sale as fertilizer.[14] The humble nature of these alternatives to teaching supports the quantitative finding that there was a large supply of potential teachers in the nineteenth century, and suggests that not all of them could find employment in their preferred role as teachers.

Information on tuition fees shows a very wide range of charges. One missionary living in east China reported that "literary men who are poor, and who fail of acquiring government employment, are frequently glad to teach school at almost a nominal price." [15] Arthur Smith, a missionary in north China, wrote, "It is not uncommon to meet teachers who have but one or two pupils, and who receive for their services little or nothing more than their food." [16] Comparison of the fees with what we know of incomes in the nineteenth century suggests that education was within the means of a rather wide social spectrum.

Literacy was also stimulated by the availability of cheap books. China, the country that invented printing, had a vigorous commercial printing industry by the thirteenth century, when private printers flourished in the urban centers, but true large-scale printing may have emerged only in the sixteenth century. Although movable type printing was known to the Chinese, it was not much used and was indeed not very convenient because of the nonalphabetic nature of the language. Woodblock printing, which dominated the industry, was a very simple and cheap method especially suited to Chinese ideographs. The major expenses were raw materials (paper, ink, and woodblocks) and the labor for transcribing, carving, printing, and sewing the sheets together. No complicated and expensive printing press was required: all of the essential tools could be packed and carried on a workman's back. Once the woodblocks were carved, printing was swift, and one man could turn out several thousand copies of a block in one day.[17]

In Ch'ing times, the printing industry was very specialized and diverse. Scholarly projects were the special concern of scholars and officials, who collected and reprinted rare editions that greatly stimulated Ch'ing intellectual life. The elite book market was dominated by firms located in the lower Yangtze delta on the east coast, in the cities of Nanking, Soochow, and Hangchow. Cheap popular editions were produced by printers in south China and by bookstores with regional branches.[18]

The onset of mass printing in the sixteenth century stimulated development of vernacular literature and produced the great eighteenth-century novels. There were collections of street ballads from different regions, immense collections of popular songs, short stories, collections of jokes, travelogues, even salacious pseudohistories of the imperial bedchambers. Morality books articulated popular religious sentiment and showed how even a relatively poor man could win spiritual merit through his everyday action. Popular encyclopedias gave advice on household affairs, sample forms for different kinds of documents and letters, arithmetic manuals, and other practical information. There were cartoons, printed in one or many colors, that were direct forerunners of the modern comic book. There were tabloid newspapers (hsin-wen-chih), sold on the streets for a few cash and designed for "the clerks, artisans, and tradespeople whose occupations required a small command of characters, and for the large numbers of men who had started on the road to scholarship and public office but stopped in elementary stages."[19] These broadsheets supplemented the officially printed gazettes to be found in

Peking and the provinces which dealt with appointments, promotions, and government affairs.

Increased printing made educational texts more widely available and at cheaper prices than ever before. By Ch'ing times, primers, Confucian texts, and other educational aids existed in great profusion. One could even purchase books presenting examination questions and winning essays.[20] There is no doubt that mass printing helped expand the base of literacy in Ch'ing society.

Schools

The Ch'ing dynasty financed a hierarchy of schools which was integrated with the examination system, beginning with schools at the county level and culminating in the Imperial Academy in Peking. These schools were only for already advanced students who had passed a series of competitive written examinations. Their private counterparts, the academies (shu-yuan), were also centers for advanced learning.[21]

Many families in the nineteenth century paid for the education of their sons. Boys born into well-to-do households might begin to read and write at home when they were only two to five years old. Since their parents or relatives were literate, instruction was informal and sometimes administered by mothers and aunts. In these early years, a boy learned to recognize approximately two thousand characters and to write a smaller number, so that by the time he was enrolled in formal studies with a tutor (between the ages of five and seven) he had already passed through elementary schooling.

Sons from households in more modest circumstances attended schools run by teachers in their own homes or in village temples. Villagers might get together to invite a teacher to set up classes: the inclusion of contract forms for this purpose in the popular "encyclopedia of daily use," almanac-like compendia that circulated widely in China, suggests that this was a common practice.[22]

Village schools were open most of the year but closed during the peak of the harvest season when students were needed to help in the fields. For those who could not afford to attend year-round schools, there were short-term courses, with fees paid daily instead of monthly or annually. These were frequently held during the winter months when the labor demands in agriculture were at their nadir.

The length of schooling a boy received varied with the means of his family. Missionaries in the early nineteenth century reported that "the better course of common education occupies the student five, six, or seven years; others are continued at their books for three or four years; while some remain only a few months, or at most one or two years. The rich generally give their sons the advantage of a full course. . . . The middling classes, of the better sort, usually give their children every aid in their power. The poor, for the most part, are restricted by their poverty from giving their children any education, or from continuing them in school beyond two or three years." [23]

Boys from families too poor to pay tuition were not necessarily barred from the classroom. Lineage schools and public charitable schools were founded primarily for this group. We know about lineage schools from the regulations concerning their operation to be found in genealogies. These schools, financed from corporate revenues, were of two types: those open to all boys in the lineage and those intended for the instruction of fatherless boys or poor lineage members. Classes would be held in part of the ancestral hall or the headquarters of the charitable estate. Such schools were probably most common in central and south China, the regions of greatest lineage strength. [24]

We know about the financing and operation of charitable schools from the detailed school regulations that have survived in local gazetteers. The schools obtained revenues from landed and other endowments. They charged no tuition and were generally open to all; sometimes the regulations state that only the poor should be admitted. The government encouraged such schools even though it did not provide funds for their establishment, so local officials were often leaders in promoting them. Contributions came from the literati and from ordinary citizens. Such schools were found throughout the empire but did not exist in large enough numbers to affect education in more than a marginal sense. [25]

Curriculum and Teaching Methods

The first lessons in school are probably universal: "When a child enters school, have him first learn to sit, to be quiet, to recognize characters; these are the lessons for the youngest in the elementary school." But there was also emphasis on observance of the Confucian ethical code: ceremonies honoring Confucius and in some cases the Neo-Confucian philosopher Chu Hsi (1130–1200) were conducted at regular intervals by the teacher and his students. Lineage schools occasionally substituted reverence before ancestral tablets for the Confucian ritual.[26]

Then there was the relationship between teacher and student, one of the most sacrosanct in the Confucian world. Education included learning the proper modes of respect toward one's teacher, expressed in daily ceremonies marking the beginning and end of classes.

Classes taught reading and writing but rarely arithmetic. Writing lessons were separated from reading lessons. Learning to write was somewhat complicated for Chinese. The first lessons were in handling the writing brush and grinding ink. The holding of a brush was demonstrated by the teacher, who would grasp the child's hand and go through the motions of writing. Children first inked over large characters written in red, then traced over them, a pedagogical method that goes back to the Sung (960–1279). It was at this stage that stroke order was taught.

In the next stage, written models were copied, often on "squared paper," so that the proper proportions of character elements within a given ideograph could be learned. Students were taught to write in the regular style (k'ai-shu), generally considered the basic foundation of writing. The number of characters assigned would be gradually increased as students progressed, to perhaps one hundred a day.

Students could practice writing on a "whiteboard," described by Doolittle: "The Chinese have boards of various sizes and thicknesses, painted white, which they often use to write upon. . . . Pupils in schools use such boards, of only half an inch thick, and six or eight inches long, by three or four inches wide, on which they practice writing Chinese characters . . . . or on which the teacher writes characters for them to see or copy." [27] Such boards could be readily wiped clean with a wet cloth or paper.

The first reading lessons might use small lacquered wooden boards, inscribed with the *Thousand Character Classic,* one character to a block. The child could learn a few characters a day; the advantage of the blocks was that they could be shuffled, arranged in different sequences, and reviewed as an educational game. In one lineage school, these blocks were inscribed with the twenty-four models of filial piety. Another first reader provided the characters to be learned in ruled squares, with common homophones on the back.[28]

The number of characters that could be absorbed in one day ranged from ten to several tens of characters. Even if we assume that a child learned only ten new characters a day, he would thus learn two thousand characters within the first year of school. These characters were learned partly by using the square blocks described above and partly by reading elementary textbooks designed to teach character recognition.

Three texts dominated elementary education. They were the *Trimetrical Classic,* the *Thousand Character Classic* and the *Hundred Names.* The *Trimetrical Classic* was the primer with which many boys began their studies. The original was written in Sung times, but by the Ch'ing many different versions were in use. The text consisted of approximately 356 lines of three characters each, and contained five hundred unique characters after repetitions are eliminated. Its famous opening lines present a basic Confucian tenet: "Men at their birth are naturally good. Their natures are much the same; their habits become widely different. If foolishly there is no teaching, the nature will deteriorate." [29] The primer blended factual and historical information with strictures on the reciprocal obligations of parents and sons, teachers and students, elders and juniors.

The oldest of the three primers, the *Thousand Character Classic,* introduced one thousand characters in 250 lines without repeating a single character. This tour de force of writing resembled the *Trimetrical Classic* in content. The third primer, the *Hundred Names,* consisted of four hundred family surnames, but since some were more than one character in length, the book actually contained over four hundred characters.[30]

When put together, these three books provided the beginning student with knowledge of about two thousand characters (eliminating repetitions) and constituted the vocabulary acquired by boys from elite families before enrolling in formal studies with tutor. The three books were also used in village and charitable schools, where they could be read in a year. They were used not because they were entertaining—indeed, the *Hundred Names* was merely a list—but because they introduced appropriate characters to beginning readers in convenient and compact form.

The three primers were essentially collections of characters. Their use in the initial phases of the elementary curriculum is explained by one scholar as reflecting the nature of the Chinese language. Without an alphabet, a child could not begin to read immediately; characters had to be learned one by one. In this first stage, emphasis was put on character recognition rather than complete comprehension, and reader interest was a secondary consideration. To begin teaching character recognition through whole sentences, thus improving the content of early lessons, would expose the child to many repetitions of characters but relatively few characters within a limited time span. At the same time, the content of the materials would have suffered from the restricted reading vocabulary the child had mastered. The use of the *Thousand Character Classic.* The *Trimetrical Classic,* and the *Hundred Names,* made possible a "crash course" for learning a certain number of characters within a short period. The student was then equipped to handle materials where content was important.

Similar considerations help explain why the reading and writing lessons were separate. Chinese students did not write the characters they learned in the reading lessons but used other materials presenting very simple characters. This was because the characters in the three primers were of varying difficulty and had not been selected for simplicity of construction. To expect beginners to start with the texts of the three primers would have made writing lessons quite difficult. Moreover, the initial pace of learning to write was slower than the pace that could be achieved in learning to read. At a later stage, progress in these areas, and in explication of texts, which was not emphasized in the early lessons, might be reversed. Traditional methods of reading and writing instruction thus recognized certain problems inherent in the nature of Chinese and compensated by presenting materials in a sequence that shifted emphasis among the goals of reading, reading comprehension, and writing.

After learning the first two thousand characters, at age seven or so, a boy in an elite household was enrolled in formal studies with a tutor. He would begin study of the Four Books: the *Analects,* the *Great Learning, Mencius,* and the *Doctrine of the Mean.* These would be followed by the Five Classics: the *Book of Changes,* the *Book of History, Book of Songs, Book of Rites,* and the *Spring and Autumn Annals.* These texts were the heart of a Confucian education.[31]

The lineage and charitable schools sometimes modified this elite curriculum for their own purposes. Many taught students who would not go on to study for the examinations. As one writer pointed out, "Farmers and the poor do not have far-reaching ambitions; they do not expect their sons to do more than several hundred characters and roughly know the meanings."[32] Very bright students might be pushed into advanced study, but for the most part, these schools were not classrooms for future degree holders.

Modification of the elite curriculum came from another direction as well. The elite were extremely interested in using schools as channels for ideological indoctrination: "When a boy understands righteousness, he can transform the elders of his household, and can transform a neighborhood." [33] Yet the elite texts were not the most effective way to inculcate Confucian values into the children of the poor, who could not spend the long years in study that so effectively indoctrinated the elite itself. The question was how to transmit Confucian values to the general populace in clear and simple terms within a relatively short time. The Four Books and Five Classics were works of profound philosophical import, written in difficult language and expressing concepts that children could not be expected to understand. None of these classics was written for children or for specific use as an elementary text. It is not surprising that when they were first studied, emphasis was put on memorization rather than on understanding. Those who were concerned with moral indoctrination saw the deficiencies of such books as primers.

Since study of the Four Books was extremely slow, in sharp contrast to the brisk pace at which recognition of the first two thousand characters was taught, there was a need even in the elite curriculum for texts that would provide simpler readings to review characters already learned as well as to teach facts and ethical principles. A wide range of books was available to fill this need. Unlike the classics, they were generally written in simpler language, some in the vernacular. Many were organized into rhymed couplets or matching paired phrases that could be chanted and readily memorized. As a school regulation observed, "These books are clear and easily understood so that ignorant people's children can all know the principles in them and adopt these in their conduct." [34]

Such books were often introduced into the school curriculum. They included texts like the *Primer of Virtuous Men in the Past* (Hsien-hsien hsiao-hsüeh), which presented role models for students to emulate; *Children's Discourse* (Hsiao-erh yü), a popular work presenting proverbs in rhyme, many in the colloquial language; *Rhymed Primer* (Hsiao-hsüeh yün-yü), or the *Rules for Youths* (Ti-tzu Kuei), a popular text that was concise, had relatively few characters, and combined catchy rhymes with simple text. [35]

Chinese classrooms also stressed explanation and repetition after the initial crash course in character recognition. "In elementary education, it is most important to explain; this method avoids learning without comprehension; when [texts] are explained in detail, there will be benefits." [36] This emphasis on reading comprehension was a dominant theme in schools.

First of all, as regulations for a lineage school pointed out, all books used in the classroom should be punctuated and carefully written so that the characters were clear. This was necessary because "there are three stages in reading books; to the mind, to the eyes, to the mouth. If it has not reached the mind, then the eyes will not read with care. If the mind and eyes are not together, the recitation will be wild and it will not be retained, or if it is retained, it will not be for long." [37] The teacher must make sure that each character is clearly enunciated and the correct meaning understood: "In all recitations, whenever there is a doubtful point . . . take advantage of the opportunity to look into it. Make sure it is understood before letting it go. If it is not answered at once there is the worry of forgetting. It is best to write it down when it occurs in a book on doubtful points which students can use for explanations." [38]

Repetition was emphasized: "One must read it over so many times that it naturally rises to the mouth, and will not be forgotten for a long time." [39] This called for regular review of materials. One regulation notes, "Take care that the readings are thoroughly familiar, the meaning understood. Every morning explain the general meaning, have them [the students] repeat it; after three days have them repeat it again, to see whether or not they remember." [40]

In writing lessons, students turned from learning to write characters to lessons on composition and style. They had to learn to write in the formal style (wen-yen) as opposed to the colloquial or vernacular style (pai-hua), which was not used for official or business communications in the Ch'ing period. One method used to bridge the gap between the written and vernacular styles was to assign students the task of rendering materials from one style to the other: "It is not necessary that they first compose; merely take one or two simple phrases and cause them to be lengthened or shortened. Take characters which have been taught and have them rendered in the vernacular; or take colloquial sayings and have these put into the literary style. Take *wen-yen* and have it put into colloquial language, or point out an object or incident to write up." [41]

The daily class schedule included a great deal of review, recitation, reading, and writing. One school's regulations state, "For each student, create a lesson book, one a month; each day carefully note in it the few characters to be learned, the few lines to be learned, the several pages to be reviewed, the few characters in the 'regular style' to be written, and the several pages of text to be explained." [42] The class day began with a review of previous work. New reading lessons were introduced in the mornings when there would also be recitation. Lunch was followed by writing practice and lectures by the teacher, as well as by more reading instruction and review.

Lectures were a means of providing moral instruction. In one school, the teacher was told to expound selected passages from morality books. He should sit at a table where students could gather around to look and listen: children like illustrated books and while they delight in the pictures, the moral of the story slips easily into the ear and the mind. In another school, selected daily passages providing moral instruction were assigned as writing lessons. The teacher took the best written example to paste on the classroom walls.[43]

Investigation of Chinese classroom methods suggests that at its best, teaching did not rely solely on memorization. Rote memorization was especially important in the initial stages of reading a text. Subsequent lessons went over texts that had been memorized to emphasize and ensure understanding. Both reading and writing lessons used repetition interspersed with exercises and recitation.

Classes were generally small. One lineage school noted that, "Since we are only hiring one teacher at present, we cannot have too many students; the number is fixed at ten." Another, which also limited classes to ten students, observed that "if there are too many, the teacher will not be able to look after them all, and the teaching will be ineffectual." [44] In charitable schools, classes seem to have been larger. A survey of the available information shows an average of twenty-three students per class in these schools.[45]

Each child within a class was allowed to proceed at his own pace, and children of varying levels would be seated within a single classroom. We have vivid accounts by missionaries of the noisy scene that ensued since each student recited his own assignment out loud. As Smith wrote, "The consequence of so much roaring on the part of the scholars is that every Chinese school seems to an inexperienced foreigner like a bedlam." [46] From the Chinese point of view, the advantage of this system of individual lessons was that students who had been absent could easily resume studies upon their return. School schedules were geared to local festivals and agricultural demand for labor. In the twentieth century, when a modern school system based on Western models tried to replace the older educational system, these aspects of the traditional school were identified by many Chinese as assets and reasons for clinging to the old rather than espousing the new schools.[47]

Uses of Literacy

The population of nineteenth-century China can be classified into several groups in terms of possession of literacy skills. At the top of the society there were the fully literate degree holders and officials. These were the Chinese literati. Literacy was fundamental to most aspects of literati life and culture. The education of sons was mandatory for persons in this group, for the family's prospects rested on the ability of each generation to acquire advanced education and win degrees and office.

Below the literati, there were men who had attended school for a few years. This group might include merchants, artisans, shopkeepers, landlords, and well-to-do peasants who tilled their own land, as well as some priests and monks. Since most elementary schools followed the orthodox curriculum, these men had studied the Confucian classics, at least in a rudimentary way. Some were forced to abandon their studies for want of funds, others were sent to work for want of academic talent. Whatever the cause of their interrupted education, persons in this group could probably read and write several thousand characters, enough to aid them in business and in land management. Aware of the value of education, these men tried, as their means permitted, to send one or more of their sons to school. While the ultimate goal was success in the civil service examinations, these men used their literacy to amass wealth in everyday life. Along with the literati, this group supported the market for popular literature of all kinds.

Then there were others who attended school for shorter periods, perhaps during the slack agricultural season. Unlike the previous group, these men were frequently not exposed to the orthodox elementary school curriculum. Their limited education did not provide sufficient basis for academic advancement. Their course of study provided mastery of probably only a few hundred characters. This enabled them to keep simple accounts and cope with small market transactions, but most probably consulted the more literate members of their communities for help in complex matters.

Finally, there were the many men and women who were illiterate. While their inability to read and write left them at a disadvantage in Chinese society, illiterates had access to information in written materials through their literate relatives and friends. The literate culture that surrounded them was orally transmitted by recitations of storytellers both professional and amateur or through the drama performances staged at important religious festivals in village and city, when heroes derived from Chinese history played out the important themes in Chinese culture. Visits to the periodic market, gossip with itinerant peddlers and with friends in the ubiquitous market teahouse provided even the rural dwellers with regular information about the world outside his own village. Lineage ties bound literate and illiterate kinsmen together, as did the enduring ties of native place and ancestral veneration.

Nineteenth-century Chinese lived in a culture which required written communications even at the level of popular religion, where requests for rain, personal aid, or foreknowledge frequently took forms paralleling official communications within the bureaucracy. Divination, another popular religious activity, also frequently took written form. And it was the almanac that enjoyed the widest sale of all books, because it provided not only climatological information for agriculture but magical guidance for daily life.[48]

The decorative element of Chinese writing also penetrated deeply into all social strata. Calligraphy was an art form favored by the literati, but everyone wrote or purchased written couplets to adorn their homes, particularly at the New Year. Characters were inscribed on windows, rocks, clothing, fans, snuff-bottles, tobacco-pouches and fan-cases; characters ornamented cups, saucers, plates, chopsticks, teapots, incense-burners, and cabinets. The appreciation of Chinese characters as decorative elements thus extended into the mainstream of Chinese culture.[49] And it is fair to say that there was virtually no aspect of Chinese culture and no group within Chinese society that was not touched by writing.

Many of the conditions promoting literacy and education in modern societies existed in late imperial China. There was government encouragement of education, recognition that it was a key element in promoting an orderly society, and attempts to reach all groups within the society. Private motivation for education was high, reflecting widespread identification of education as the means of achieving upward mobility both in terms of entry into the bureaucracy and in terms of trade and local influence. Ch'ing society was governed by a bureaucracy through detailed, written regulations, so ordinary people were aware of the significance of literacy as a necessary tool for coping with government and with a complex society. Because ties to native place kept Chinese elites returning to rural villages, and since the elite curriculum was well defined, there was an integrated curriculum throughout the empire and a demand for schooling in rural as well as urban places. These factors all played their part in producing the relatively high rates of pre-modern literacy prevailing in nineteenth-century China.

Notes

1. Joshua Dukes Edwin, *Everyday Life in China; or, Scenes Along River and Road in Fuh-kien* (London: The Religious Tract Society, n.d.), pp. 194–95, 196, 198.

2. Sidney Gamble, *Ting Hsien: A North China Rural Community* (New York: Institute of Pacific Relations, 1954), pp. 185–86.

3. Arthur H. Smith, *Village Life in China* (1899; reprint ed., Boston: Brown, 1970), p. 202.

4. Kwangtung province, for example, seems to have enjoyed high levels of female literacy: see John E. Reinecke, *Language and Dialect in Hawaii: A Sociolinguistic History to 1935* (Honolulu: University of Hawaii Press, 1969), table 12, p. 120. Nineteenth-century estimates of female literacy are found in *Chinese Repository* (1832–33):306, 2(1833–34):252, 4(1835–36):7, 6(1837–38):234.

5. *Chinese Repository* 2(1833–34): 252.

6. Evelyn Sakakida Rawski, *Education and Popular Literacy in Ch'ing China* (Ann Arbor: University of Michigan Press, 1979).

7. Ping-ti Ho, *The Ladder of Success in Imperial China* (New York: John Wiley and Sons, 1964), pp. 179–94.

8. Agnes Smedley, *The Great Road: The Life and Times of Chu Teh* (New York: Monthly Review paperback, 1972), pp. 14–15, 36–45.

9. Rawski, pp. 9–11.

10. Rawski, pp. 13–15; Wang Hui-tsu, *Hsüeh-chih i-shuo*, cited in Etienne Balazs, *Political Theory and Administrative Reality in Traditional China* (London: University of London, School of Oriental and African Studies, 1965), p. 56.

11. Myron Cohen, in an introduction to Smith, *Village Life*, p. xv.

12. P. T. Ho, *Ladder of Success*, p. 314.

13. Rawski, pp. 96–97, appendix 1, 2.

14. P. T. Ho, *Ladder of Success*, pp. 36–37, 303; Yu-wen Jen, *The Taiping Revolutionary Movement* (New Haven: Yale University Press, 1973), pp. 30–31. Feng was eventually rescued from his lowly occupation and hired as a private tutor.

15. Justus Doolittle, *Social Life of the Chinese—with Some Account of Their Religious, Governmental, Educational and Business Customs, and Opinions, with Special but not Exclusive Reference to Fuchau* (New York: Harper, 1865), 1:61.

16. Smith, *Village Life*, p.52.

17. Rawski, pp. 119–23.

18. Ibid., pp. 115–18.

19. Roswell S. Britton, *The Chinese Periodical Press, 1800–1912* (Shanghai: Kelly and Walsh, 1933), p. 6; Britton describes (p. 4) how newspapers were printed on clay blocks and wax blocks that could be cut more quickly than wood and later reused.

20. P. T. Ho, pp. 214–15; on printing of examination papers, a practice that began in the sixteenth century, see K. T. Wu, "Ming Printing and Printers," *Harvard Journal of Asiatic Studies* 7 (1943):250.

21. The government schools are described by Chung-li Chang, *The Chinese Gentry: Studies on Their Role in Nineteenth-Century Chinese Society* (Seattle: University of Washington Press, 1955), pp. 4–5, and P. T. Ho, *Ladder of Success*, pp. 169–73. On Ch'ing academies, see P. T. Ho, *Ladder of Success*, pp. 200–203.

22. Rawski, pp. 24–28.

23. "First Annual Report of the Morrison Education Society," *Chinese Repository* 6(1837–38):235.

24. Rawski, pp. 30–32.

25. Ibid., appendix 1.

26. In *Meng-hsüeh lu,* cited in Ch'en Tung-yuan, *Chung-kuo k'o-hsüeh shih-tai chih chiao-yü* (Education in China's scientific age) (Shanghai: Commercial Press, 1934–35), p. 50. Rites of Confucius are described in *Chinese Repository* 2(1833–34):250.

27. *Social Life,* 2:385.

28. Rawski, pp. 46–47.

29. Chang Chih-kung, *Ch'uan-t'ung yü-wen chiao-yü ch'u-t'an* (A preliminary study of traditional language primers) (Shanghai: Shanghai Educational Press, 1962), pp. 16–21, 158–59. The translated lines are from Herbert A. Giles, *Elementary Chinese: San Tzu Ching* (Shanghai: Kelly and Walsh, 1910).

30. Chang Chih-kung, pp. 6–10, 11–16, 21–25, 154–58. The explanation offered in subsequent paragraphs of the text is from Chang Chih-kung, pp. 32–36.

31. The program of study for those preparing to take the civil service examinations is described by Ch'en Tungyüan, pp. 52–59.

32. *Shang-ch'eng hsien-chih* (Gazetteer of Shang-ch'eng county), 1803 edition, 6.3b.

33. Regulations for charitable schools, in Yü Chih, *Te-i lu* (Records of a purist) N. p., 1869, *chüan* 10.3, .1ab.

34. School regulations in *Chih-chiang hsien-chih* (Gazetteer of Chih-chiang county), 1870 edition, 12.41ab.

35. Rawski, pp. 50–51.

36. T'u clan rules, reprinted in Taga Akigorō, "Shinmatsu kakyo haishi zen sōzoku keiei no gakkō kyōiku ni tsuite" (Late Ch'ing education in clan-managed schools before the abolition of the civil service examinations), *Kyōiku shigakkai kiyō; Nihon no kyōiku shigaku* 1(1958):92–125.

37. *Jun-tung Piao-lin Chu-shih t'ung hsiu tsung-p'u* (Revised genealogy of the Chus of Piao-lin, Jun-tung), 1846 ed, 1.3b–4a.

38. *Yün-shih chia-ch'eng (Yün genealogy),* 1859 ed., 1.22b, 1.24b.

39. *Jun-tung Piao-lin Chu-shih,* 1.3b–4a.

40. Lu clan regulations, reprinted in Taga Akigorō 8, *Sōfu no kenkyū* (Investigations of clan genealogies) (Tokyo: Tōyō Bunko, 1960), pp. 586–87.

41. *Hsü-chou fu-chih* (Gazetteer of Hsu-chou prefecture), 1874 ed., 15.17b.

42. Ku clan regulations, in Taga Akigorō, *Sōfu no kenkyū,* p. 585.

43. Ibid., pp. 584, 586, 587.

44. The Lu family genealogy in Taga, ibid., p. 587, T'u genealogy and Yao genealogy in Taga, 'Shinmatsu kakyo," pp. 120–21, n. 32; pp. 118–19, n. 26, all cite ten students as the maximum.

45. Rawski, table 2, p. 42.

46 Smith, *Village Life,* p. 82.

47. Rawski, pp. 162–67.

48. J. J. M. de Groot, *The Religious System of China* (1892; reprint ed., Taipei: Literature House, 1964), 5:905; on the almanac, see C. K. Yang, *Religion in Chinese Society* (Berkeley: University of California Press, 1967), p. 17.

49. J. J. M. de Groot, "Inscriptions on Red Paper, Pictures etc. on Chinese Street-doors," *The China Review* 9 (1880–81):20; W. H. Medhurst, *The Foreigner in Far Cathay* (New York: Scribner, Armstrong, 1873), pp. 144–45.

Schooling and Literacy in
Late Imperial Russia

by Ben Eklof

Ben Eklof is a specialist in nineteenth- and twentieth-century Russia and the Soviet Union at Indiana University in Bloomington. He has published articles on Russian popular education, the Mir, and teachers before and after the Revolution. He is preparing a book on the late Imperial Russian school system.

In this chapter, Professor Eklof revises our understanding of popular education in the Russian countryside before the Revolution by stressing its sources in the peasant effort to learn and use the skills needed to maintain an existing and vital rural culture. To support this argument, he draws heavily on survey material gathered by the Tsarist Ministry of Education.

The history of literacy and education in late Imperial Russia is a largely uncharted field, despite a fabulous abundance of sources. There is, for example, no satisfactory history of the humble, rural primary school. It has been virtually ignored in favor of the secondary schools and universities that were producing the radical culture which allegedly led to the Revolution. Yet, a study of primary schooling, its interaction with peasant culture, and its successes in developing reading, writing, and numeracy skills can make an important contribution to our understanding of the relationship of formal education and functional literacy. At the same time, this kind of study is closely linked to one of the major concerns of late Imperial Russian historiography, the continued vitality of the Russian peasant commune, which dominated the lives of 80 to 90 percent of the population.

In 1864, three years after Alexander III's emancipation of the serfs, landmark legislation provided guidelines for the establishment of primary schools in the Russian Empire and allowed considerable private initiative in their construction and support. Other legislation that same year established, in thirty-four provinces, local institutions of partial self-government called zemstvos, which, though democratically elected, remained elite units dominated by landowning nobility. The zemstvos were encouraged to look after local needs and were given responsibility for the primary education of peasants under the jurisdiction of the Ministry of Education.[1]

Until the 1890s, however, and despite the 1864 legislation, elite support for primary education was halting at best. Because zemstvo assemblies were dominated by the gentry, whose children were educated in existing urban schools or by tutors, they had no personal interest in educating peasant youth. To the contrary, they showed strong vestiges of traditional elite hostility to mass education even after the Emancipation of the Serfs. Moreover, considerable evidence suggests that, in order to launch a broad drive for peasant education, the gentry would have had to increase taxes on their own grossly under-assessed lands to levels like those at which peasants were taxed. Few were willing to do this. Instead, they alleged that the peasants themselves were unwilling to vote funds for school construction.[2]

The fact is, however, that a study of basic schooling and literacy suggests that before the 1890s, the main support for schools and the spread of literacy came from the peasants, not from the elite zemstvos. In the half-century between the Emancipation and the Russian Revolution, peasants fought hard to shape schools and schooling to meet their perceived needs, which, by the turn of the century, often differed radically from the goals of progressive educators. Although historians sometimes cite the large number of schools opened by the zemstvos in the first decades after the Emancipation as evidence of their sincere commitment to education, the figures are deceptive. (The number of schools and enrollments did rise impressively between 1856 and 1896, but in the late 1880s the peasants still paid 30 percent of teachers' salaries and book costs and the full cost of facilities.) As late as 1893, only one out of ten schools was wholly funded by zemstvos. And because zemstvo educational revenues were obtained largely from land taxes based on arbitrary assessments that forced a grossly disproportionate share of the tax burden on the peasants, it can be said that peasants sponsored not only their own but the gentry's education.[3] Furthermore, though zemstvos are credited with establishing a large number of schools before 1890, many of these "new" schools were already existing but unofficial (thus unrecorded) peasant schools merely taken over by zemstvos.[4]

Peasant support and development of their own schools has been largely obscured not only by these views of the zemstvo's role, but also by attention paid to a protracted and far-reaching struggle among competing elites for control of the growing network of primary schools. By the end of the nineteenth century, there were more than thirteen types of primary schools in the Empire; the main rivals for their control were the Ministry of Education and the Holy Synod. Separate local school boards were established to administer schools under these two branches of the government, and from 1884 to 1894 imperial favor seemed to rest with the parish rather than the secular schools. Yet, by the beginning of the twentieth century, the schools under the Ministry of Education had gained an absolute majority of enrolled pupils, and from that time on their dominance was assured. By 1911, the Ministry controlled 59.5 percent of all schools and 68 percent of enrolled pupils.[5] Of all the rural schools under the Ministry's control, the most dynamic ones, by this time, were those run and sponsored by the zemstvos.

Nevertheless, although the zemstvos and other private or semiprivate institutions were encouraged to fund and maintain schools as well as to hire teachers, the Ministry sought to maintain tight control. The curriculum was set down by the central government, teachers were subject to approval (or dismissal) by local inspectors, and a complex web of regulations governed nearly every detail of school affairs. The zemstvo private school offered three years of instruction, generally by a single teacher in a one-room schoolhouse. The course of instruction included reading, writing, and arithmetic as well as Bible study and Church Slavonic. These schools were for all practical purposes terminal, because, in order to continue his education, a peasant would have had to transfer to the six-year urban advanced primary school for another three years of study before he could be admitted to secondary school.

Elite attitudes toward popular education changed considerably in the 1890s and gave rapid rise to a major commitment of new funds and energy for primary education in the countryside. This change can be explained in large part by the shock waves generated by the major famine that hit much of Russia in 1891–92 and by the changing of the guard after the death of Alexander III in 1894. The relief efforts that followed the famine, which the press saw (perhaps unjustly) as government ineptitude and callousness, began a decade of widespread agitation for the extension of political freedoms. The wave of political energy crested in the Revolution of 1905–7, after which it subsided, leaving a shaken but intact political structure.

One demand upon which all forces seemed to agree was for universal primary education. In 1897 a delegate to the Kharkov zemstvo said:

> Poverty and ignorance—here are the main reasons for all our ills. Which of these two sores is worse it is difficult to say, we are only sure that they are tightly and inseparably connected and causally interdependent; we are poor because we are ignorant, and ignorant because we are poor—how can we escape this vicious circle, which ill should we cure first? [6]

The concern for public education became so widespread in the 1890s that enrollment rates and per capita expenditures on education came to be regarded as the best measures of a country's strength and the level of civilization attained by its people. Relentlessly the message was driven home: If too much education was dangerous for the unsophisticated, too little education was dangerous for the nation's health. As in the West, the assumption that literacy and progress are identical became dogmas of progressive thought, but also reached deeply into conservative governmental circles.

Now, as we shall see, it was the zemstvos that mounted the most sustained drive for education. The turning point clearly came in the period 1894–97 when, after three decades of granting minimal attention to primary school concerns, the provincial zemstvos through the country actively took up the cause. During these three years, twenty-four zemstvo assemblies took up the question of universal education; seventeen of these actually undertook systematic statistical work to determine the state of education in their provinces, and twenty set up special loan and grant funds for the construction of schools. An even clearer signal of their serious intent was the establishment of permanent school commissions in twenty-three provinces and school bureaus (by 1908 there were some nineteen) in nearly all the rest. By the end of the century, many provincial zemstvos had accepted the responsibility of offering loans and subsidies for the construction and maintenance of schools, for supplements to teachers' salaries, for school libraries, and in some cases for school breakfasts and night lodgings for pupils who otherwise could not attend school. In turn, the principle of free education, initially accepted by Moscow and only a few other provinces, was now nearly universally recognized.[7] By 1911, in the thirty-four provinces where zemstvos operated, some forty-six thousand teachers were working with just over 2 million rural schoolchildren.

Now it is possible to step back and inquire into the causes of this fundamental change in attitudes throughout elite society, causes compelling enough to prompt to immediate action a society fond of debate and idle projects. Many historians have alluded to the famine of 1891–92 as the explanation for the 1890s stepup in activity. The resulting "democratic movement," so the argument goes, had to recruit the peasants into the struggle against the tsar, and the only way the peasant could participate intelligently in politics was if he were educated.

Certainly many who were politically active in Russia had learned from John Stuart Mill that basic education was prerequisite to democracy, and there were even more who drew the same lesson from the writings of Jules Simon, a popular if sententious contemporary French educator. It is at least partly true that the zemstvos "approached the problem of elementary education in the spirit of nineteenth-century European liberalism." [8] Still, it is hard to read the journals and conference papers of the day without coming away with the impression that other, more powerful forces were at work. In fact, what was emerging was a confluence of forces promoting general education as a solution to the core of problems we often associate with the transitional phases of modernization. Some saw the problem as one of labor productivity and labor discipline; some perceived it as one of agricultural output and techniques. Still others believed that only literate conscripts could efficiently handle modern weapons and fight modern wars. An article on elementary education in the prestigious Brokgaus-Efron Encyclopedia stated boldly that it was Prussia's devastating victories over Austria (1866) and France (1870) and the widespread belief that "the Prussian schoolteacher was responsible for the victory at Sedan" which helped push through the English school reforms of 1870 and contributed to the passage of the 1874 Military Statute in Russia.

This thought remained in the minds of educators in the early twentieth century. The *Popular Encyclopedia,* published by Russia's magnate of the popular press, Sytin, for the new reader, stated in the introduction to the volume on education that Japan in 1904 had five times as many teachers for every hundred people as Russia did and concluded: "from these figures it is clear why the 'Asiatics' defeated us: they are better educated than us!" [9]

In the 1890s, both zemstvo and government expenditures for education rose sharply, relieving the peasants of the heaviest burden for building and maintaining schools. Between 1894 and 1914, zemstvo outlays for primary education rose from 7.7 million to 104.7 million rubles. And government expenditures rose from 1 or 2 percent of the budget in the mid-nineteenth century to more than 7 percent by 1914. Almost half of the central government's education budget went to primary education. In all, the government spent 61,460,000 rubles building schools and another 54,900,000 rubles subsidizing existing zemstvo schools between 1909 and 1915. The shift in emphasis from secondary to primary education came at the same time that the total budget of the Ministry of Education was expanding rapidly and signaled an important change in official attitudes and strategies.[10] Yet, despite this investment, Russia, in 1910, lagged far behind western Europe in percentage of the eligible population enrolled in primary schooling and in outlay per pupil (see Table 1).

Clearly, local and federal governments had launched an enormous campaign to spread primary education and, except for WWI, would have reached the overwhelming majority of school-age children in the Empire within twenty-five years. What should not be forgotten, however, is that, before the political and economic changes of the 1890s, progress in primary education was largely the result of efforts by peasant communities.

Now it is possible to examine the actual successes of the Russian school system before 1914 and to attempt to gauge peasant response to formal education. The study of the impact of formal schooling upon a community actually involves a cluster of problems. The most basic—and problematic—is the impact of literacy upon the mind. In this context, scholars have recently emphasized the existence of various stages of literacy, each marked by a different set of limiting abilities. That is, learning *to read* must be distinguished from learning *from reading*, rote recitation of familiar texts from reading with comprehension.[11] Reflecting the concerns of Russian primary schools, most government surveys in the last decades before the First World War tried to gauge only the most basic levels of literacy, involving either rote recitation or the ability to sign one's name. These studies, and official records registering the number of schools and the rate of enrollment of school-age children, provide us with data on the literacy achievement as well as the limitations of Russian primary schooling.

An examination of this data shows that the ratio of enrolled to eligible school age children rose impressively during the last half-century before World War I. By 1915, 51 percent of all school-age children were enrolled in publicly supported schools. But other data on early withdrawals and the length of school attendance suggest that the child's contact with the school environment and the teacher was hardly long enough to promote a high degree of literacy and to complete the normal three-year program. After the 1890s, most provinces considered only eight- to eleven-year-olds (as opposed to seven- to thirteen-year-olds) eligible, and the law of 1908 providing funds for zemstvo schools to accelerate the drive for universal enrollment required that those districts receiving funds also accept this more modest definition of eligibility. The proportion attending a school varied drastically from province to province [12] (see Table 2).

Nonetheless, our findings lead us to believe that perhaps two out of every three army recruits, three out of four residents in St. Petersburg, and with regional variations, one or two out of ten women in the countryside could "read"—that is, could recite a familiar text—or could affix their signature to a document. We know from zemstvo, military, and government surveys that these people "were able to form the letters of their own signature, or to link sets of letters with the corresponding parts of spoken words." For knowledge about what proportion possessed the "ability to understand an unfamiliar text . . . transferable learning, generalized understanding, or reasoning skills,"[13] we must turn to other sources. One, in particular, responds specifically to our questions about the extent to which higher levels of literacy skills had been reached.

Until 1906, the armed forces offered reduced terms of service for those recruits who met certain educational qualifications. For recruits who had completed the basic three years of primary school and passed the certifying examinations offered at the end of three years, the term of service was reduced from six to four years. There can be no question that successful completion of the examinations indicated that the testee had achieved the stage of comprehensive literacy, for the regulations stipulated that:

> A candidate must . . . be able to read fluently, correctly, and intelligently a narrative or descriptive passage from an unseen book in the Russian or Slavonic character, and to reproduce the subject matter in response to questions: must write from dictation correctly and with due regard to punctuation, and be able to read manuscript: must work common problems in the four primary rules of arithmetic, and show a knowledge of Russian weights and measures, coinage, and divisions of time.[14]

The portion able to read and answer questions "from an unseen book," to take one of the examination criteria, was very low, despite the remarkable rise in primary school enrollments. Within the entire Russian Empire, the portion registered as functioning at that level remained below one in ten (see Table 3). The portion of recruits who qualified for reduced terms through examination success was far lower than the portion enrolled in schools but came close to representing those who had had a full three grades of instruction.

One explanation for the low literacy achievement registered in the military examinations must lie in the school experience of the majority of the rural conscripts. Our data indicate that few of those enrolled in primary schools actually remained there for a minimum of three years. In Moscow (the province, not the city), for example, fewer than two in five of those actually enrolled in schools entered the third grade. Even with the spectacular rise in enrollments (from 53 to 82 percent of the eight-to-eleven age group) which took place in Moscow province in the last decade before the war—only 10 percent of the school-age population (eight to eleven) managed to complete the meager three-year program. The figures for Moscow, despite the considerable resources devoted by that province to primary education, were surprisingly typical of the pattern in the other zemstvo provinces. In Moscow—by 1914, the leading province in Russia in per capita outlays on elementary schools—the distribution of students by grade remained virtually the same as in 1896 [15] (see Table 4).

For the bulk of the school-age population, elementary education consisted of a little over two years of schooling (a little less for girls than boys) in classes which held from forty to sixty pupils. Those who enrolled had very irregular attendance patterns. Many students arrived at school some two months late, after the harvest was in, and left early to help with the spring planting, while others couldn't brave the elements of winter— either because of the distance they had to travel or lack of warm clothing. It is hard to imagine how teachers, who had to coordinate the activities of three grades simultaneously in the same physical setting, also succeeded in integrating the late-comers and early leavers. Although the school year nominally lasted between 140 and 170 days (from September to May in the industrial provinces, from October to April in the agricultural provinces), the teacher seldom had more than four or five months to work with most students. Whatever the case, it is clear that most "enrolled" children spent not three years, but one or two sequences of five to six months in the rural school—with six-month intervals between, in which to forget everything they learned! [16]

Why did parents take their children out of school? During the 1890s, studies conducted in several provinces left little doubt that economic conditions prevented a large percentage of the

112

population from attending even the existing schools. These studies established a direct correlation between school attendance and the size of family land and livestock holdings, and they demonstrated that up to 66 percent of all early withdrawals were prompted by reasons "of a purely economic nature." In a highly influential study of Kherson province, N. Borisov wrote that "the poorest peasant households, which have no land under crops, make only infrequent use of the schools."[17]

The importance of economic factors in promoting or limiting school-based literacy was also shown in independent studies elsewhere. In 1893 I. P. Bogolepov, the renowned educator, statistician, and zemstvo employee, with the help of a team of trained fieldworkers, carried out a study of eight hundred villages in two districts that were as different as night and day in population density, communications networks, local employment and—perhaps most interesting—amount of money per capita allocated by the local zemstvo to primary education. Bogolepov, after a detailed study of enrollment figures and withdrawal rates in the two districts, came to the surprising conclusion that despite the differences in wealth and geographic location, the two school systems had many negative features in common:

> . . . although the reasons for non-attendance in the two districts are multiple, the statisitical evidence on hand uncovers the highly significant fact that the most common and overriding cause is one and the same for the relatively fortunate Moscow district and the completely destitute Mozaisk district . . . there can be no doubt that the prevalent cause of illiteracy among children of school age is to be found in economic conditions—poverty in all its aspects.[18]

One obstacle to regular attendance common to both areas was illness. Given the primitive sanitary conditions in rural Russia, children were often too feeble to make the daily trip to school. Moreover, the school itself was a place where contagious diseases could be transmitted from one household to the next, and parents were often reluctant to send their children to such centers of disease. This was particularly true where the school buildings were maintained by the peasant commune rather than by zemstvo subsidies, and where heavy overcrowding and overuse increased the incidence of disease.[19]

In reality, the relationship between "economic conditions" and school attendance was complex. Although periods of industrial boom drew children out of the schools for employment, by the first decade of the twentieth century only a small fraction of the school-age population (3 to 4 percent) worked in factories; and most of those taking factory jobs did not do so until they were fourteen or fifteen. Certainly farm work and employment in local cottage industries, more than work in factories, competed with the schools for the child's time,[20] and it is reasonably clear that parents carried out rude calculations of the opportunity cost of education. How much the *family* would gain by a continued education was set against the likely loss in labor or earnings. In many cases, a family would send only one child to school, estimating that one literate member was enough to serve the family's needs. A second would be sent to the factories, and the remaining children would stay home to tend the farm and work in local cottage industries.

Because families tended to think of schooling in terms of the needs of the entire household, parents seemed to feel that while literacy and numeracy were essential skills, a complete elementary education might "ruin" their child. The investment in such an education would quite likely be lost to the family, as the "lettered" child would be more likely than not to leave the village for an administrative or clerical job. There is much evidence to suggest that while peasants recognized the tremendous importance of literacy and numeracy for material success in a world increasingly crowded with written instructions, correspondence, mathematical computations, and money exchange, they also chose to limit the exposure of their children to the school system.

The very mixed sentiments of the peasantry on the subject of schooling are not easily quantifiable, but they run like threads through the frequent reports sent by local correspondents (often teachers) to the zemstvo educational bureaus. Here is a sample:

> Even the poor peasant makes sure that his sons are literate, for today an illiterate wouldn't even be given a job as a *dvornik* [doorman] . . . but many children don't wait until the final exams . . . the parents take them out [of school] saying "we have no need of an examination, our children won't be clerks."

> The peasants in our regions are engaged in a brisk trade and acutely feel the need for literacy. Every family keeps up a cottage industry, and the account books must be maintained . . . the demand made of the school, incidentally, is minimal, that "the boy can read a bit," make out a letter, "write a note," this explains why few pupils reach the senior division and why, as soon as they can read and write freely, they leave the schools.

The path taken by the contemporary school in order to develop the mental faculties of the peasant children is not fully comprehended by the locals. Although they recognize the usefulness of schools, a lot of what is taught is considered a necessary evil to be suffered through in order to gain the ability to read and comprehend what is written, and to count.[21]

These descriptions also suggest why the parents of many peasant schoolchildren were often impatient with and suspicious of "progressive" readers and primers introduced after 1900, that made use of folk and fairy tales for reading lessons. Many peasants frowned on the stories used in these primers, calling them "entertainment, a waste of time, and frivolous." The emphasis was upon utility: time is money, the muzhik seemed to say. "You can learn *skazki* [tales] without knowing how to read—better to spend your time learning something useful." [22] Ushinsky's tales of animals so irritated many parents that they refused to let their children do the assigned homework.

Indeed a major point of controversy between educators and the official bureaucracy at the turn of the century was the 1897 Model Program adopted by the Ministry of Education, which limited the curriculum of the elementary school to basic reading, writing, arithmetic, Church Slavonic, and Bible lessons. While progressive educators wanted to include geography, history, and natural science as formal courses and rid the schools of what they saw as the turgid and scholastic textbooks recommended by the Ministry of Education, parents seemed to be indifferent or even to prefer the model program. In Perm, local correspondents to the zemstvo, when asked if the peasants were happy with the "existing organisation of the schools," reported overwhelmingly (78.6 percent) in the affirmative; another 7.1 percent reported indifference, and only 14.3 percent noted dissatisfaction. In those instances where dissatisfaction was observed, this was often linked with regressive illiteracy: the child soon lost the meager skills he had acquired and was unable to compose a letter, understand written documents, or read out loud to his family. Peasants, however, did not blame the official curriculum for this slippage; instead they complained that their children soon forgot the basics because the schools "spent time on trifles [*izlishye*] on stories about pigs or dogs," and taught "songs and fairy tales." [23]

The course content of privately organized peasant primary schools in the villages, very numerous in some provinces, offers indirect confirmation of this argument. Since parents paid individually to keep their children in these schools, and these schools generally remained free of supervision, they had a direct say in the books used and the subjects taught. An extensive study of these schools carried out in Tver province in 1888 showed that out of every ten teachers, four had no formal education and four others had been educated only in zemstvo or parish primary school. The curriculum was therefore likely to follow the basic program advanced by the ministry. From a study of another district in the same province, it is clear that the textbooks were generally limited to ABC books, breviaries, and psalters.[24] It would be wrong, however, to infer that parents actually chose religious over secular books, for the Holy Synod worked actively to spread religious works to the countryside and often subsidized their cost.

Peasant attitudes toward education for their children were far from uniform. When asked what specific benefits peasants saw in education, the Perm correspondents presented a surprising variety of answers: [25]

Peasant's reasons for sending a child to school

(775 answers)	Percent citing reason
Literacy regarded necessary for everyday life to compose and read documents, keep records, etc	21.4
Education as a "cultural broadening"	18.1
Military benefits	16.8
Literacy considered necessary to fulfill elective communal obligations and for various other public affairs	16.6
Literacy brings material advantages	14.6
Literacy necesssary to satisfy religious needs and duties	7.7
General utility of literacy	4.8

The table tells us that a large majority of peasants found the ability to read and write necessary simply to cope with life at the turn of the century. Thus, the utility of education was seen as much in terms of survival as advancement. The table also suggests, we must admit, that there were families in the countryside who saw the achievement of "culture" as an end in itself and were apparently not afraid of the effect of this culture on their children. That said, it should be noted that less than one-fifth of those surveyed were placed in this category.

Finally, the table suggests how little importance religion per se had in promoting literacy. Compared to the Protestant countries, where the call to draw inspiration directly from the Bible was at one time perhaps the single most important reason for widespread popular literacy, in Russia there was little or no connection between literacy and the religious impulse (with the major exception of the Old Believers). Certainly the fact that the Orthodox Bible continued to be printed in Old Church Slavonic rather than modern Russian discouraged the establishment of such a link.

The dominant utilitarian concern for education among the peasantry, however, generated little interest in educating girls:

> Why should we teach our girls, ask the peasants. They won't be taken as soldiers; nor as clerks in the stores. They're too busy to read books. On weekdays, they work at heavy labor side by side with their men, either in the fields, the woods or in the garden. They have an equal amount of work waiting for them at home, preparing meals for the family, tending the cattle, taking care of the family and sewing the clothing. On holidays, they are busier than ever! [26]

Frequent references to prevailing mores, in curt answers such as *ne priniato, ne zavedeno* or even *mody net,* (all meaning roughly "that isn't the way it's done") reflect the fact that at least as late as the 1890s literacy was not seen as appropriate for girls. The family was concerned primarily with marrying the daughter off and, as one peasant sardonically noted, literacy was not considered a notable addition to the dowry. Another provided a simple explanation of the notion of opportunity cost—"If you send the girl to school, you spend money; if you don't—she brings money home!" [*obuchat' devushku, znachit raskhodovat'sia, ne obuchat'-poluchat' barysh'.*] There were even reports that if a girl were sent to school, the neighbors and even the village elder might accuse the parents of shirking the communal tax burden and impose a supplementary tax, or *nakidka,* on the unfortunates. Bogolepov indicated that it was those families or villages engaged exclusively in agriculture which objected most strongly to the education of girls. The utility of education was seen in terms of the ability to keep accounts, read letters, and recite from the prayer book, and when the head of the family (or *bol'shak*) was home throughout the year there was no need or reason for the peasant woman to read.

When peasants saw a specific use value for the family in educating one or all of their children, they were prepared to make sacrifices to that end. By the turn of the century it was generally accepted that in order to function in society males simply had to be able to read and write. Despite the general peasant prejudice against female education, this was true in specific cases for girls, too, particularly when the husband was away for six months or more working in the factories or when account books had to be kept. The orientation of this education was practiced. It seems clear that the peasants—at least the parents—did not agree with the basic tenet of Russian progressive education. This tenet, stated first by Pirogov in the 1860s and reaffirmed in an influential article by Bunakov in the 1890s, was that education's purpose was to prepare the student for life rather than for a trade.[27] The peasants wanted their children to bring useful tools away from the schools, and felt they could prepare their own children for life, thank you!

Basic numeracy was also a concern of both the peasantry and the schools. According to zemstvo studies carried out between 1895 and 1900 the primary schools spent five hours a week on arithmetic. It is not difficult to find out what the teacher was expected to put across, for the examination conferring reduced terms of military service was very specific in its demands. The examinee had to know "the first four functions (addition, subtraction, multiplication, division) and be able to apply this knowledge to simple practical tasks encountered in everyday life." He was also required to "have a clear notion" of Russian measures of length, weight, time, of liquid and dry substances, and of monetary units." Model lesson plans to accomplish these tasks in the primary grades have also been preserved.[28]

Basic mathematics instruction in the village, however, was a complicated matter for the peasantry. Traditionally, the Russian peasant had little use for official weights and measures, relying instead on local systems of calculation. For example, when the peasant spoke of his land, he seldom talked in terms of linear or square measurements. Instead, he referred to the number of *shares* he held, a share being a proportion of the communal land, determined by the number of able-bodied workers or mouths to feed (*edoki*) in the village. Fields were divided into *uchastki* and *iarusy* measured by sticks, and uneven strips were further divided into *kliny, kortyl'ki, zamerki, otseki, shirinki, platuski*—terms designating a specific contour and land quality but having no absolute measurable value. This peasant stick (variously called *kol'verevka, shag,* and *lapot'*) bore no correspondence to the official unit of measurement, the *sazhen'* or *desiatina*.[29] For the vast majority of students, the units of measurement taught in the school were not those they encountered in everyday life.

What were the peasants learning in the school system? If we are to believe the numerous alarms sounded in the press, regressive illiteracy was a widespread phenomenon, and it was not uncommon to meet graduates of the primary schools who, ten years later, could not read a word and could barely sign their own names. The shortcomings of the system were naturally blamed upon government interference and rigid control over curriculum.

However, during the 1890s, a number of tests of graduates of the zemstvo schools were carried out in an effort to measure the degree of retention five to ten years after completing the school program. The tests were not coordinated; some were carried out through the mail, others by special teams of inspectors, and still others by individual teachers. Nevertheless, the students tested numbered in the thousands, and the results were surprisingly uniform.[30] Graduates of the schools, and even those who did not finish, were learning to read, and often with comprehension. *Pismennost'*, the ability to write correctly, was harder to find among former pupils.

In many areas, there were reports that reading speed and comprehension had improved since graduation; nearly everywhere primary school graduates had little difficulty in reading simple texts out loud and restating them orally in their own words. Retention of Church Slavonic was satisfactory, perhaps because the gospel and psalters were inexpensive and widely circulated. Ability to carry out simple math calculations varied considerably from region to region. Everywhere the lowest scores were given on *pis'mo*, or composition; what was being tested, however, was logical sequence of thought and style, not rudimentary writing. In the one study where true recidivism was tested, it was found that only 12 out of 1028 could no longer write simple sentences. In short, according to these surveys, graduates of zemstvo schools had learned how to read, write, and count, and were retaining those skills.

Despite the finding that most of the school graduates could write simple sentences, some local studies uncovered serious problems with spelling and grammer. A Kursk study of 720 former pupils showed that 35 percent could not spell their own name correctly. In six to seven lines of dictation, improper knowledge of word boundaries was observed in 50 percent of the sample, word distortion in 29 percent, omission of hard or soft signs in 34 percent. By far, the worst area was with the redundant Church Slavonic elements in the orthographical system, such as the letter *jat'*, which 64 percent of the pupils used incorrectly. This letter and hard *jers*, which caused so much trouble, were eliminated with the orthographic reforms of 1917 (the hard *jers* was dropped at the ends of words, but retained medially);

what is important here is that these troublemakers were of little or no semantic importance. Word distortion may be a sign of the persistence of local dialects, and the high level of improper word separation suggests a low degree of familiarity with the written word. However, in only 20 to 25 percent of the cases were the written compositions given failing grades and judged fundamentally incoherent.[31]

The personal observations of one educator, who had close knowledge of four districts (two agricultural and two industrial) over a span of five years, provides further support for the argument that the schools were doing their job—if the job was to teach the basics:

> Graduates of the public schools are able to recite by heart the most commonly used prayers, but knowledge of the text is seldom accompanied by the ability to retell the content in everyday language; they are able to give a brief exposition of the main events from the Old and New Testaments; they have mastered the core of the Orthodox service and the basic concepts of the Orthodox catechism; this last amounts to the assimilation, as far as this is possible for children aged eleven to thirteen, of the basic dogmas of Orthodox teaching, and only rarely to a conscious grasp and understanding of the foundations of Christian morality; in general, the ethical side of Christianity is poorly assimilated by students in our primary schools; in their Bible lessons, their attention is completely riverted on the factual, ritual and dogmatic side. The graduates . . . can read in Church Slavonic the less difficult passages in the Gospels and provide a free translation into modern Russian. They can freely and easily read from anthologies (in Russian) of suitable content, or passages from any book in the school library, and can provide an oral or written exposition; they can take a brief dictation from the teacher, again of suitable content; in dictation or written exposition they display the ability to avoid gross transgressions of the rules of orthography. In arithmetic, they are able to carry out all the functions with variables as well as numerals of any magnitude and to solve problems with these numerals on paper; orally, they can solve problems using all four functions with numbers up to a thousand.[32]

Of course, the biggest shortcoming of these tests was that they examined only graduates of the schools who had by definition completed the entire program. As we know, this represented only a small fraction of enrolled pupils; obviously regressive illiteracy would be much higher among the early dropouts. It is true that the educator Bunakov, who worked a lifetime in the countryside, claimed that he could teach children to read in three months, but he also noted a high degree of regressive illiteracy among former students in his school. At this time the question of retention of school learning by the mid-course dropouts must remain open. This should not obscure the point that the school program as it was designed was offering the skills which the peasants needed for everyday life; the information which disappeared entirely (history, geography, natural science) was also that which contained the cultural baggage most inimical to the peasant way of life.

The zemstvo correspondents also studied peasant attitudes towards advanced elementary and secondary education at the turn of the century and just before the war. While there were impressive gains in the portion of students of peasant background who could be found in the secondary schools and universities, these gains altered little the individual peasant's real chances of pursuing an education. Throughout Russia only one out of nine children who completed their basic elementary education or slightly more than one in two hundred peasant children actually continued his education, and the vast majority of this number simply proceeded to the advanced elementary school for a few years of additional instruction.[33]

Why didn't the peasants continue with their education? The opportunity cost of keeping a child between the ages of twelve and fourteen in school must have been quite low—except in cases where work in cottage industry was available or when an adolescent was needed to watch after young siblings while the parents were out working. In fact a number of reports suggested there was some interest in the construction of advanced elementary schools where employment in local cottage industries was not available. As one commentator put it: "the peasants finish school at thirteen and have to chase dogs for two years until the factory will take them." The 1911 countrywide zemstvo survey of education reported a surprisingly high level of interest among local population in building more advanced schools. Some even saw schools as a possible antidote to the apparently rising rate of delinquency.[34]

However even the reports of individual correspondents gathered in 1911 speak of at best a mixed attitude towards advanced education. From Saratov, we read that: "Many local residents look at advanced education from the business point of view, they are prepared to make outlays on education for their children, but only with the guarantee that the money isn't simply thrown away (*ne propali zria*)."

The obstacles on the road were formidable. Since all advanced elementary schools were located in towns or cities, and charged fees, the outlays on tuition as well as room and board were considerable, even prohibitive for all but the wealthiest peasant families. It was precisely the prospect of a lost investment to the family which discouraged peasants from sending their children to these schools. To be sure, the child who made his way into the world of service occupations and retained a degree of loyalty to family might be in a position to send money home. In areas where land was short and hands plentiful, the investment might have seemed justified. But the risk was also high. As one Perm correspondent expressed it, the peasant child was likely "to shove off from one shore, but not make it to the other (*ot odnogo berega otstanet a k drugomu ne pristanet*)."

From Moscow, we read:

> If you send your children to study in the advanced schools, you're likely to end up with neither peasant nor lord, (*ne muzhik, ne barin*); they become ill-adapted for agricultural work but fail to gain a better position in life.

Another villager wrote:

> A fellow, during his stay at the (advanced) school, becomes unaccustomed to farm work, but with this education alone, it is almost impossible to find work with his mind. The result? As the saying goes, Matryena became neither a beauty nor a crow (*i sdelalas' Matryena ni pava ni vorona*).

To many peasants, the indigent village teacher was a striking example of the dubious reward of education: "Before their eyes they have the flagrant example of the impecunious teacher who, having studied his fill, now receives 20 rubles a month compared to his peers who, with nothing but elementary education, earn two or three times more than the teacher."

But parents were sometimes just as fearful of the success that education might bring. From Ekaterinoslav we read that the parents "fear higher (advanced elementary) education as a means of alienating a member of the family from the patriarchial conditions of domestic life . . . they look at the educated son as some kind of *barin*, incapable of hard work, and they can expect no support for themselves in old age." The limited available evidence of a statistical nature confirms that those who did complete an advanced elementary education, including study at agricultural schools, overwhelmingly left the villages, and even agriculture, to pursue low level white collar occupations; as far away from the hearth as possible, one suspects! [35]

It is somewhat more difficult to find evidence justifying parental fears that a complete basic education would also send the child in search of a "soft vacancy," as a Perm study labeled the problem. One historian has recently examined migration patterns to the city of Moscow and concludes that literacy was not a determining variable.[36] In Perm, only 38 of 631 correspondents noted that a "significant number" of graduates from the elementary school left agriculture. This same study indicated that the degree of knowledge attained was insufficient to gain access to official service (*sluzhba*) even as a lowly village clerk. The striving to leave the village was most prominent among former military recruits and individuals from large families. But perhaps it was just this striving rather than actual movement which made parents unhappy, caused generational friction, and prompted some peasants to turn away from schools which offered "Learning with a capital L" (*bol'shaia nauka*) or had particularly inspiring and dedicated teachers to the parish schools run by the clergy and offering only two years of no-nonsense training in the ABC's. One suspects that regional differences in landholding, occupation, family size, and tradition also played a major role.

Thus, the peasant response to education was a complicated one, based overwhelmingly on considerations of utility and opportunity cost but clearly not on ignorance. Certainly, there is reason to suspect that the peasants' strategy for their children was one of gaining the tools of literacy and numeracy while minimizing the impact of the school system on their culture. Yet the evidence available suggests that those who completed the basic program, and perhaps, too, those who stayed only a year or two, were coming away with the reading and writing skills necessary for survival, if not mobility, in peasant society.

Notes

1. See E. N. Medynskii, *Istoriia russkoi pedagogiki* (Moscow, 1938), pp. 264–69; also Baron N. A. Korf, *Russkaia nachal'naia shkola* (St. Petersburg, 1871)—the handbook on primary education which inspired a generation. The best work in English on the 1864 School Statute and subsequent legislation is T. Darlington, *Education in Russia*, Great Britain: Special Reports on Educational Subjects, vol. 25, (London, 1909). Although early Soviet works lambasted the zemstvos and dismissed their activities as insignificant, a recent major work is very unguarded in its praise of zemstvo education work: A. I. Piskunov, ed., *Ocherki istorii shkoly i pedagogicheskoi mysly narodov SSSR: Vtoraia polovina XIX v.* (Moscow: Pedagogika, 1976), p. 68.

2. See, for example, B. B. Veselovskii, *Istoriia zemstva za sorok let* (St. Petersburg, 1909–1911), vol. 1, p. 527. For a

more thorough discussion of these issues, see my article in the *Slavic and European Education Review*, "The Village and the Outsider: The Rural Teacher in Russia, 1864–1914," (1979, no. 1) pp. 1–20.

3. C. Charnoluskii, *Zemstvo i narodnoe obrazovanie*, 2 vols. (St. Petersburg, 1910), vol. 1, p. 68; B. B. Veselovskii, *Istoriia zemstva*, vol. 1, p. 471; George L. Yaney, *The Systematization of Russian Government* (Urbana: University of Illinois Press, 1973), p. 348.

4. On *vol'nye* or *"free"* schools, see especially A. S. Prugavin, *Zaprosy naroda i obiazannosti intelligentsii v oblasti umstvennogo razvitiia i prosveshcheniia* (Moscow, 1890), pp. 31–52; also, N. V. Chekhov, *Tipy russkikh shkol v ikh istoricheskom razvitii* (Moscow, 1983), pp. 28–34.

5. N. V. Chekhov, *Narodnoe obrazovanie v Rossii* (Moscow, 1912), pp. 222–23.

6. Cited in *Narodnaia entsiklopediia*, (Moscow, 1911–12), vol. 10, p. 62.

7. Chekhov, *Narodnoe obrazovanie*, p. 220: Veselovskii, *Istoriia zemstva*, vol. 1, p. 516; vol. 3, p. 389; vol. 4, p. 6; *Narodnaia entsiklopediia*, vol. 10, p. 64.

8. Robert H. Dodge, "Peasant Education and Zemstvo Schools in the Moscow Province," *Topic:* 27, XIV (1974), p. 60.

9. Mizhuev, "Elementarnoe obrazovanie," *Entsiklopedicheskii slovar' Brokgaus-Efrona*, vol. 80, p. 623; *Narodnaia entsiklopediia*, vol. 10, p. XIII.

10. A. P. Pogrebinskii, *Gosudarstvennye finansy tsarskoi rossii v epokhu imperializma* (Moscow, 1968), pp. 19–29; Nicholas Hans, *History of Russian Educational Policy* (New York, 1964), 230–32; G. Fal'bork and V. Charnouskii, *Narodnoe obrazovanie v Rossii* (St. Petersburg, 1899), pp. 193, 194–5; Veselovskii, *Istoriia zemstva*, vol. 1, p. 32; M.N.P., *Odnodnevnaia perepis' nachal'nykh shkol rossiiskoi imperii*, 16 vols., (Petrograd, 1916), vol. 16, p. 125.

11. Daniel R. Resnick and Lauren B. Resnick, "The Nature of Literacy: An Historical Explanation," *Harvard Educational Review*, vol. 47, no. 3 (August, 1977), pp. 371–84.

12. The age at which children should be considered eligible was a source of heated dispute among Russian educators. Those who favored universal education, led by V. P. Vakhterov, defined eligibility as eight to eleven, rather than the more commonly accepted seven to fourteen. This reduced the pool from 16 percent to 6.5 percent of the population (according to contemporary estimates) and put universal education within striking distance in a generation. It also reduced the proposed outlays necessary for such a drive from 125 million rubles annually to somewhere between 10 and 20 million. Soviet historians, fond of understating the tsarist achievement in this area, prefer to use the seven to fourteen figure. If eight to eleven is considered the proper figure, then by 1915 some 51 percent of the population of European Russia of school-age was enrolled in school. See Veselovskii, *Istoriia*, vol. 1, pp. 520–22; N. A. Konstantinov and V. Struminskii, *Ocherki po istorii nachal'nogo obrazovaniia v Rossii.* (2nd edition, Moscow, 1953), pp. 186–87; I. M. Bogdanov, *Gramotnost' i obrazovanie v dorevoliutsionnoi Rossii i SSSR* (Moscow: Statistika, 1964) pp. 24–25, and especially E. O. Vakhterova, *V. P. Vakhterov, ego zhizn' i rabota* (Moscow, 1961), pp. 255–98; A. G. Rashin, "Gramotnost' narodnoe obrazovanie v XIX i nachale XX v.," *Istoricheskie zapiski* (XXXVII, 1951), p. 69. For the 1908 Law, see *Polnoe sobranie zakonov Rossiiskoi Imperii* (3rd Series), 1908, vol. 28, #50328.

13. Resnick and Resnick, *The Nature of Literacy*, p. 379. The 1897 census defined as literate all those who responded affirmatively to the simple question, "Can you read?"

14. See *Polnoe sobranie zakonov rossiiskoi imperii* (2nd Series), vol. No. 52983; Thomas Darlington, *Education in Russia*, Special Reports on Education Subjects,

vol. 23, (London, 1909), pp. 249–52. Guidelines for the examinations may be found in A. S. Prugavin, *Zakony i spravochnye svedeniia po nachal'nomu narodnomu obrazovaniiu*, 2nd ed., (St. Petersburg, 1904), pp. 1008–22. These privileges were discontinued in 1907: N. Verigin, *V pomoshch' uchashchim v nachal'nykh uchilishchakh*, 5th ed., (Moscow, 1915), p. 148. For a description of how the examinations were actually conducted, see Bunakov, *Sel'skaia shkola i narodnaia zhizn'* (St. Petersburg, 1906), pp. 34, 183–94. The translation is Darlington, p. 239.

15. V. Trutovskii. *Sovremennoe zemstvo* (Petrograd, 1914), p. 74; "Obzor narodnogo obrazovaniia," in *Statisticheskii ezhegodnik moskovskoi gubernii za 1915* (Moscow, 1916), p. 207; Biuro obshchezemskogo s'ezda narodnomu obrazovaniiu, *Trudy*, vol. 6; *Svodka svedenii* (Moscow, 1912) 6, table 3, p. 7 (hereafter: *Svodka svedenii*). In 1906 the Moscow province schools turned away 1136 children for lack of space; in 1914, 1,769. See "Obzor narodnogo obrazovaniia," *Statisticheskii ezhegodnik . . .* (Moscow, 1915), p. 204.

16. V. Akimov, "Postanovka uchebnogo dela v zemskikh shkolakh," *Zhurnal Ministerstva narodnogo prosveshcheniia* (new series, 62; 1916, no. 3), pp. 55–57; Bunakov, *Sel'skaia*, pp. 210, 37, 183–90. Bunakov claims, p. 15, that by using the phonic method he could teach students arriving in September or even October the alphabet, and "to read with understanding" as well as to take dictation by Christmas. His description of a syllabus which allowed for students entering and departing at different times is on pp. 59–94.

17. V. I. Charnoluskii, *Zemstvo i narodnoe obrazovanie*, 2 vols. (St. Petersburg, 1910), vol. 2, p. 337; V. A. Kumanev, *Revoliutsiia i prosveschchenie mass* (Moscow: Nauka, 1973), pp. 44–48, 68.

18. I. P. Bogolepov, *Gramotnost' sredi detei shkol'nogo vozrasti v moskovskom i mozhaiskom uezdakh moskovskio gubernii* (Moscow, 1894), p. 21.

19. D. M. Bobylev, *Kakaia shkola nuzhna derevne?* (Perm, 1908), p. 71.

20. For precise data on the proportion of children engaged in industry and in chores as well as farmwork, see Panteleimon Vikhliaev, *Vliianie travoseianiia na otdel'nye storony krest'ianskago khoziaistva*, 9 vols. (Moscow, 1908–15), vol. 9, pp. 16–30. For a lengthy discussion of sources and evidence, see my forthcoming book, *Schools and Peasants in Imperial Russia*.

21. The comments are taken from Bogolepov, *Gramotnost'*, pp. 67–68, 100–103; V.V. Petrov, *Voprosy narodnogo obrazovaniia v moskovskoi gubernii*, 4 vols. (Moscow, 1896–1901), vol. 3, pp. 2–15.

22. V. I. Orlov, *Sbornik statisticheskikh svedenii po Moskovskoi gubernii* (Moscow, 1884), vol. 9, p. 202.

23. Bobylev, *Kakaia*, pp. 82–87.

24. V. Devel', "Krest'ianskie vol'nye 'shkoly gramotnosti' v Tverskoi gub.," *Russkaia shkola* 1, (4, 6, 8, 1890), pp. 96–111, 130–47, 120–34.

25. Bobylev, *Kakaia*, p. 40.

26. The comments are taken from Petrov, *Voprosy*, 3, pp. 9–11 and Bogolepov, *Gramotnost'*, pp. 67–68, 100–103. See also Bobylev, *Kakaia*, pp. 34–39.

27. N. Bunakov, *Shkol'noe delo*, 3rd ed. (St. Petersburg, 1906), pp. 6–14; Nicholas Hans, *History of Russian Educational Policy* (New York: Russell and Russell, 1931), pp. 97–101.

28. F.F. Korolev, ed., *Ocherki po istorii sovetskoi shkoly i pedagogiki (1917–1920)* (Moscow, 1958), p. 18; A. Anastasiev, *Narodnaia shkola. Rukovodstvo dlia uchitelei*, 2 vols., 7th ed. (Moscow, 1910). Vol. 1, pp. 80–93, vol. 2, pp. 319–55; For the examination requirements, see Prugavin, *Zakony i spravochnye svedeniia*, pp. 1008–22.

29. Moskovskaia gubernskaia zemskaia Uprava, Sbornik statisticheskikh svedenii, vol. 4, book 1, *Formy krest'ianskago zemlevladenia* (Moscow, 1879), pp. 25–29.

30. See E. A. Zviagintsev, *Narodnaia zhizn' i shkola*, 2 vols. (Moscow, 1912). Vol. 2, pp. 1–29; Bunakov, *Sel'skaia shkola*, pp. 175–82; Biuro obshchezemskogo s'ezda po narodnomu obrazovaniiu, vol. 5 *Anketa uchashchim zemskikh shkol* (Moscow, 1911), pp. 61–79. (Hereafter: *Anketa*). My forthcoming book devotes an entire chapter to retention studies.

31. Zviagintsev, *Narodnaia zhizn'*, p. 24.

32. A. Bulatov, "K voprosu o retsedive bezgramotnosti," *Russkaia shkola* (December, 1907), p. 41. But see his own qualification of this statement on p. 45.

33. A.G. Rashin, "Gramotnost," pp.

74–79; *Svodka svedenii*, 7, table 33, p. 111. For a discussion of access and distribution percentage, see Fritz K. Ringer, *Education and Society in Modern Europe* (Bloomington: Indiana U. Press, 1979), p. 26.

34. N. Kazimirov, "Otnoshenie naroda k shkolam povyshennogo typa," *Statisticheskii ezhegodnik* (Moscow, 1912), pp. 77–91; *Anketa* IX, pp. 170–74.

35. The quotations are from *Anketa*, 7, pp. 115–20; Bobylev, *Kakaia*, p. 100.

36. Joseph Bradley, "Patterns of Peasant Migration to Late Nineteenth-Century Moscow: How much Should We Read into Literacy Rates?" *Russian History* (vol. 7; 1, 1979), pp. 33–34.

Table 1

Elementary Education in Selected Countries, 1910

Country	Percentage Enrolled to Pop.	Outlays per pupil in dollars	Outlays per capita in dollars
Austro-Hungarian Empire	15.7	6.18	.97
Great Britain	17.14	17.63	3.02
England and Wales	17.14	17.63	3.02
Scotland	16.86	15.09	2.54
Ireland	16.1	11.45	1.84
German Empire	17.0	12.17	2.05
France	14.2	11.92	1.40
Sweden	14.2	12.12	1.72
India	1.8	1.33	.02
Japan	11.5	3.57	.41
Canada			
USA	19.4	31.65	4.45
Mexico	5.7	5.78	.66
Chile	5.05	13.77	.69
Russia	3.85	7.34	.28

Source: U.S. Office of Education, Annual Report of the Commissioner (Washington, 1910), vol. 2, pp. 1333–41; MNP, *Odnodnevnaia perepis'*, vol. 16 pp. 2–3.

Table 2

Percentage of School-age Children (Eight to Eleven) Enrolled in Primary Schools, 1911: Selected Provinces*

Russian Empire	44.2	Saratov	61.3
34 zemstvo provinces	53.5	Kovno	21.6
Tambov Province	48.2	Vologda	45.8
Moscow Province	84.2	Irkutsk	49.3
Viatka Province	46.2	Stavropol	41.1
Archangel Province	54.0	Orenburg	30.4
Smolensk	58.5	Fergana	1.6
Bessarabia	40.3	Samarkand	2.4
Lifland	79.9	Semirech'e	9.4

* The figures include students and schools under the jurisdiction of the Ministry of Education and Holy Synod. If the scattering of schools under other ministries is included, the number of schools would increase from 93,407 to 100,295 and the number of pupils from 5,862,409 to 6,180,514. This would increase the proportion of enrolled to eligible from 44 percent to 46 percent. For a criticism of the method used in arriving at these figures, see Ia. Ia. Gurevich, "O chisle detei shkol'nogo vozrasta, ostaiushchikhsia vne shkoly," *Russkaia shkola* (no. 4,1911), pp. 93–95

Source: Compiled from N. P. Malinovsky, "Nekotorye vyvody po dannym shkol'-noi perepisi, 1911 g." *Russkaia shkola* (1911,4), pp. 74–75.

Table 3

Percentage of Recruits Eligible for Reduced Terms of Service Because of Examination Performance, 1876–96

Area	1876	1886	1896
Thirty-four zemstvo provinces	1.3	6.3	12.4
Four non-zemstvo provinces*	.8	2.8	5.5
Northwest region **	1.5	4.4	5.7
Southwest region ***	.7	2.5	5.4
Baltic region †	2.8	4.4	6.2
Tsarist Poland	1.0	.5	.6
Caucasus	.6	1.9	5.4
Siberia	1.2	2.1	5.4
Steppe region ††	2.9	3.8	3.3

* Archangel, Astrakhan, Orenburg, and the Don Cossack Oblast.

** Vilna, Vitebsk, Grodno, Kovno, Minsk, and Mogilev provinces.

*** Volhynia, Kiev, Podolia.

† Since schooling was compulsory in the Baltic, and literacy virtually universal, these low figures require further explanation. They may reflect the requirements of the test that the examinee read fluently in Russian or reflect anomalies in the administration of the tests.

†† The slight decline observed in this area (primarily Kazakhstan today) between 1886 and 1896 also must reflect differences in the testing procedures which need further clarification.

Source: Fal'bork and Charnoluskii, *Narodnoe obrazovanie* . . . , pp. 146–50, 208, 213. Unfortunately, I have been unable to locate information on recruits and examinations after 1896.

Table 4
Percentage of Pupils in Each Grade
Thirty-Four Zemstvo Provinces (1910–11)

	first	*second*	*third*
Boys	44.1	36.1	19.8
Girls	53.9	33.0	13.0

Moscow Province 1896–1911			
Boys:	*first*	*second*	*third*
1896	48	35	17
1903	43	37	20
1911	43	37	20
Girls:			
1896	60	33	11
1903	53	34	13
1911	51	35	14

Source: Pavel Vikhliaev, *Ekonomicheskie usloviia narodnogo obrazovaniia v moskovskoi gubernii* (Moscow, 1910), pp. 22–23; *Statisticheskii ezhegodnik moskovskoi gubernii za 1910* (Moscow, 1911), p. 29.

Literacy and Schooling in
Subordinate Cultures:
The Case of Black Americans

By John U. Ogbu

John U. Ogbu, professor of anthropology at the University of California, Berkeley, has done cross-cultural research on education and stratification in contemporary Africa and the United States. His publications include The Next Generation: An Ethnography of Education in an Urban Neighborhood *(New York: Academic Press, 1974) and* Minority Education and Caste: The American System in Cross-Cultural Perspective *(New York: Academic Press, 1978).*

Professor Ogbu's current work is on the paradox of high educational aspirations and low school performance among urban black Americans. This chapter criticizes some of the theories that have been introduced to explain poor performance and assesses the meaning of failure. Improvement, he suggests, will require a different structure of social rewards and incentives.

The preparation of this paper was supported by a grant from the National Institute of Education and by the Faculty Research Fund of the University of California, Berkeley. The editors of the Journal of Social History *have kindly granted permission to use in this article portions of Professor Ogbu's essay "Peasant Sloth Reconsidered" (vol. 14, no.3).*

Literacy is currently receiving a good deal of attention from researchers, policy-makers, and professional educators. Common concerns are the development of literacy among children and the problem of literacy competence or functional literacy among adults. In industrialized nations like the United States these problems are regarded as particularly acute among the lower class and subordinate minorities.

The literacy problem of subordinate minorities, the focus of this paper, is threefold and relative, the latter because it derives partly from comparing minorities with the dominant group. One aspect of the problem is that a larger proportion of minorities has not successfully learned to read, write, and compute. Another is that a greater proportion of minorities is not functionally literate. That is, they are unable to demonstrate the ability to read, write, or compute in social and economic situations that require these skills; for example, they cannot fill out job applications and income-tax forms or read and comprehend instructional manuals and utilize the information. Third, school children among subordinate minorities lag behind their dominant-group peers in reading and computation as judged by classroom grades and scores on standardized tests.

Our research since the late 1960s has been on this lag in minority student's performance, and we have compared the situation in the United States with those in other countries like Britain, India, Israel, Japan, and New Zealand. For this paper, we will limit our discussion to black Americans, beginning with the current hypothesis that black children fail disproportionately in school because they come from a predominantly oral culture which engenders a discontinuity in their participation in the literate culture of the school. We will then suggest an alternative interpretation of the disproportionate school failure of black children in its historical and structural context.

Oral Culture, Literate Culture, and School Performance

Shifting Theories of Language Research

Over the past two decades, there has been a continuing shift in theories generated by language studies to explain the disproportionate failure among blacks to learn to read. A brief review of these theories, as provided by Simons (1976), will take us to the current hypothesis that school failure among blacks, especially in reading, is due to the fact that they come from an essentially oral culture.

Initially, the field of language studies was dominated by a deficit perspective, whose hypothesis (which still survives in some quarters) is that black dialect is inferior to standard English and constitutes a handicap in the thinking and learning of blacks. Ethnographic studies by Labov (1972) and others showed that this model was false, and it was replaced by the difference perspective, whose initial hypothesis asserted that black dialect is different from standard English but still constitutes a viable system of thinking and learning. Black children failed, especially in reading, because a "mismatch between children's language and the language used in school and in the reading texts interfered with black children's acquisition of reading skills" (Simons 1976:3). That is, schools did not use black dialect as a medium of teaching and learning.

Efforts to use black dialect in texts and in the classroom, while teaching standard English, did not, however, improve reading achievement among black children. Critics charged that the difference hypothesis focused too much on materials and teachers and failed to specify the mechanisms by which the interference or mismatch occurred. Critics proposed two types of interference, the first of which was phono-logical. It was thought that differences in pronunciation "might interfere with the acquisition of word recognition skills," but this was subsequently shown not to be a significant factor (Simons 1976:8; see also Rentel and Kennedy 1972). The second hypothesized interference was grammatical; that is, a "mismatch between black child's syntax and the standard English syntax of the texts used by the teacher" (Baratz 1969; Stewart 1969). But reading achievement among black children who read materials written in black dialect grammar did not significantly improve. It was concluded from these studies that black dialect was not the source of the failure of children to learn to read (Simons 1976:11).

In the early 1970s a new hypothesis moved beyond language *per se* to the broader area of communication strategies, speculating that school failure is caused by a mismatch between communicative etiquettes of teachers and students, especially during reading. The hypothesis holds that teachers and minority students who come from different cultures have different communicative strategies and interpretations of situated meanings that lead to miscommunication during reading activities. This interferes with children's acquisition of reading skills.

What is at issue is what is *communicated* by the classroom environment, not the differences in the cultural backgrounds or languages of the teacher and students. The goal of research is to isolate the processes that are meaningful to the participants in classroom communication. Philip's notion of participant structure (1972) provides the conceptual framework for this research. Basically, a participant structure is "a constellation of norms, mutual rights and obligations that shape social relationships, determine participants' perceptions about what is going on, and influence learning" (Simons 1976). Subordinate minority-group children have different participant structures at home than at school, and their generally poor school performance is attributed to this discontinuity.

I have criticized this mismatch hypothesis (Ogbu 1980a), on three grounds. First, it does not warrant generalization about minority school failure because it is based primarily on research into only one type of minority group, namely, castelike minorities. It does not explain why other minorities, who also have different participant structures at home than at school, learn to read in the same classrooms where blacks and similar groups fail. Second, the mismatch model ignores historical and societal forces which may actually generate the pattern of classroom processes. And third, although data and insights from studies based on the mismatch model can be used for remedial efforts (Simons 1976; Erickson 1978), they cannot lead to social change that would eventually eliminate the need for remedial efforts.

Oral Culture and Literacy

The most recent development in language studies focuses on literacy and attributes the disproportionate school failure of blacks and similar minorities to a discontinuity between their essentially oral cultures and the literate culture of the white middle-class represented by the public schools. This hypothesis is based on studies of literacy and its consequences in traditional or small-scale societies (Goody 1977; Luria 1976); on studies of language and communicative styles in minority communities (Labov 1969; Abrahams 1970; Kochman 1973); and on microethnographic studies of teacher-pupil interactions in classrooms (Erickson and Mohatt 1977, cited in Koehler 1978; Gumperz 1979; Philips 1972).

Reviewing studies of both nonliterate, small-scale societies and literate Western societies, Lewis (1979) argues that participants in oral cultures differ significantly from participants in literate cultures, whose sensory orientations are aural rather than oral. She cites a large body of evidence that these two sensory orientations generate contrasting notions of time, causality, space, and the self "which affect the way children are raised and interact with adults" (p. 2). Although the contrast is primarily between non-Western nonliterate populations and Western middle-class populations, she coins the term "residual oral cultures" or "residual oral peoples" to designate segments of Western societies (e.g., subordinate minorities and the lower class) in which many people have minimal knowledge of reading and writing, arguing that these populations resemble in many respects those of nonliterate small-scale societies. Lewis claims that the disproportionate school failure of minority and lower-class children in the

United States is due to their participation in those essentially oral cultures. As she puts it,

> [In] our society, the schools as key institutions of literate culture tend to reject the oral tradition. As a result, the relatively illiterate find their assumptions about reality in conflict with school expectations. This conflict insures failure and exacerbates other experiences of race and class exclusion (p. 2).

One difficulty with Lewis's formulation is the questionable extent to which one can generalize from small-scale Asian and African societies to groups historically subordinated by their class, ethnic, and racial backgrounds in complex industrial societies. Furthermore, the introduction of literacy or schooling in the small-scale societies does not usually result in the same types of problems it often creates among subordinate minorities and the lower class in the United States (Heyneman 1979; van den Berghe 1979). To the contrary, the introduction of schooling in small-scale societies tends to increase cognitive and linguistic or communicative similarities to the pattern of middle-class populations of industrialized societies (Cole and Scribner 1973; Greenfield 1976; Luria 1976). Why, then, after generations of school attendance by blacks and centuries of interaction with whites, haven't their cognitive and communicative strategies changed to those of the white middle class?

Finally, we know that descendants of illiterate Asian and European immigrants (who might be regarded as "residual oral peoples") have achieved greater success in American public schools than subordinate minorities. For example, studies of Chinese peasant villages in the 1930s (Pepper 1971: 199; Snow 1961: 69) showed that illiteracy rates were often as high as 90 percent. But children of illiterate Chinese peasant immigrants have done quite well in American schools. Gumperz and Cook-Gumperz have proposed a sociolinguistic formulation of the problem (1979). Drawing from the work of Goody (1977) and Luria (1976), they contrast oral and literate cultures in terms of (1) storage and transmission of knowledge, (2) decontextualization of knowledge, and (3) cognitive strategies in communication and learning. They argue (1) that in oral cultures stored knowledge is static and its transmission inaccurate, whereas in literate cultures change is built into knowledge and its transmission is accurate; (2) that knowledge acquisition and transmission in literate cultures, unlike oral cultures, are decontextualized; and (3) that in literate cultures a distinctive mode of reasoning emerges that is separate from everyday activities. Using these three domains of change as criteria, the authors contend that the *home,* in contrast to *school,* is a place of oral culture, and they suggest the changes children must make in their cognitive and communicative strategies in order to learn and use written language effectively. They summarize the process involved in the transition from oral to written culture for all children as follows:

> Developmentally the transition from speaking to writing as a medium for learning about the world of others requires a change from the interpretative strategies of oral cultures in which children grow up, to the interpretative principles of discursive written language. The move into literacy requires children to make some basic adjustments to the way they socially attribute meaning to events and the processes of every day world in order to be able to loosen their dependence upon contextually specific information and to adopt a decontextualized perspective. Among other things, they must learn to rely on an incrementally acquired knowledge rather than on what is said within any one context. In another dimension the move into literacy requires children linguistically to change their process of interpretation (p. 16).

Gumperz and Cook-Gumperz imply that literacy problems began in the present century with industrialization, bureaucratization, and other socioeconomic changes which have tended to (a) erase the boundaries between elite and popular education; (b) increase the dichotomy between speaking and writing; (c) make literacy prerequisite to economic survival; and (d) institute evaluation of literacy competence through methods which take no account of the socioeconomic changes (Gumperz and Cook-Gumperz 1979:11–12).

If this twentieth-century situation creates problems for all children, why do some children make the transition to literacy more easily than others? According to the authors, some oral cultures prepare children better than others: "The argument we have been developing," they state, "is that for all children the literacy experience requires essential changes in the processing of verbal information. For some children, however, the shift of understanding of written language is sometimes facilitated by early language experience; the child is able early in life to gain processing experience of the written word" (p. 27). Elsewhere, after reviewing several microethnographic studies of communicative interaction between teachers and children of subordinate groups (e.g., Native Americans, blacks, Native Hawaiians, rural Appalachians, and working-class British), Gumperz sums up the underlying cause of their disproportionate school failure as follows:

> This work highlights the point that children's responses to school tasks are directly influenced by values and presuppositions learned in the home. It demonstrates moreover that classroom equipments, spatial arrangements or social groupings of teachers and students are not the primary determinants of learning. What is important is what is *communicated* in the classroom as a result of complex processes of interaction between educational goals, background knowledge and what various participants perceive over time as taking place (1980:5).

The authors have certainly made an important contribution to our understanding of the cognitive and linguistic changes all children make in learning to use written language. But their implicit and explicit explanations of the special problem of minorities is essentially one of mismatch of communicative etiquettes which we previously criticized. Furthermore, in looking at the problem historically, we find that the educational experiences of blacks and other subordinate minorities in the United States (e.g., Chicanos, Indians) do not conform to the nineteenth century situation described by the authors (Ogbu 1978). Though many Americans idealize education for its own sake, for most Americans, and for blacks in particular, it has been aimed at developing marketable skills. We shall return to this point later.

The oral culture-literate culture discontinuity hypothesis seems inadequate to explain the disproportionate school failure of subordinate minority children. We shall suggest an adequate hypothesis which considers both historical and macro-structural forces that shape classroom processes under which children acquire their literacy. But first we wish to distinguish subordinate minorities from other minorities who do not necessarily share similar problems in school and from lower-class people for the same reason.

Stratification as a Context: Castelike & Class

We define a given population as a minority group if it is in a subordinate power relation to another population in the same society. A minority status is not determined by mere number because the subordinate group might outnumber the dominant group, as the Bantu in South Africa outnumber whites by more than 2 to 1. For some purposes, such as education, it is useful to distinguish different types of minorities, and in our work we have classified minorities into autonomous, castelike and immigrant types.

Autonomous minorities, which are represented in the United States by Jews and Mormons, are also found in most developing Asian and African nations. They are primarily numerical minorities who may be victims of prejudice but are not totally subordinated in systems of stratification, and their separateness is not based on specialized denigrated economic, political, or ritual roles. Moreover, they often have a cultural frame of reference which demonstrates and encourages success in education and other areas as defined by the larger society.

Castelike Minorities—those we have referred to as subordinate minorities—are either incorporated into a society more or less involuntarily and permanently or are forced to seek incorporation and then relegated to inferior status. In America, for example, blacks were incorporated through slavery; Chicanos and Indians through conquest.

Castelike minorities are generally regarded as inherently inferior by the dominant group, who thus rationalize their relegation to inferior social, political, economic, and other roles. Until recently it was (and in many instances still is) more difficult for castelike minority-group members than for dominant-group members to advance on the basis of individual training and ability. The concept of a job ceiling (Ogbu 1978) at best describes the circumscribed occupational and economic opportunities historically faced by castelike minorities. A job ceiling is set by the pressures and obstacles that consign minorities to jobs at the lowest levels of status, power, dignity, and income and meanwhile allow the dominant group to acquire the jobs and rewards above those levels. As we shall argue, the access of castelike minorities to schooling and their perceptions of and responses to schooling have historically been shaped by the job ceiling and related barriers.

Immigrant minorities are those who have come more or less voluntarily (unless they are refugees) to their new society for economic, political, and social self-betterment. Immigrants may be subject to pillory and discrimination but have usually not internalized their effects. That is, at least in the first generation, they have not experienced such treatment as an ingrained part of their culture and thus have not been disillusioned to the same extent as castelike minorities. This is true even when the two minority types are faced with the same job ceiling and other barriers. Immigrants also tend to measure their success or failure against that of their peers in their homeland and not against the higher classes of their host society. (See Ogbu 1978, for further elaboration of these and other factors that differentiate immigrants from castelike minorities.)

Minority groups do not usually accept subordination passively, though their responses vary. Some groups reduce or eliminate aspects of their subordination; others may actually reinforce some aspects of that subordination. Moreover, different types of minorities respond differently. Except for political emigres, the immigrants have the symbolic option of returning to their homeland or re-emigrating elsewhere. This option may, in fact, motivate the acquisition of education and literacy because immigrants can transfer these skills elsewhere for greater rewards. Because this option is usually not open to castelike minorities, they tend to develop various gross and subtle devices to raise, eliminate or circumvent the job ceiling and other barriers. We shall explore the important implications that these devices have for schooling and literacy.

Lower-Class and Castelike Minorities

Current discussion tends strongly to equate the education and literacy problems of castelike minorities with those of the lower class. But the differences between them appear in the attempt to distinguish castelike stratification from class stratification. "Caste" or "castelike" in this essay is a purely methodological reference to the structural form underlying the history of minority subordination in America and similar societies.

In a class stratification people are ranked by their education, their jobs, their behavior and how much money they make; that is, by achieved criteria. Lower-class individuals have difficulty advancing into higher classes by achieving more wealth and education or better jobs and social positions because they lack requisite training (education), ability, or proper connections. But class stratification, at least in the United States, has a built-in ideology which encourages lower-class people to strive for social and economic self-betterment that would put them and/or their children into higher classes. This social mobility occurs enough among white Americans that they view America as a land of great opportunity and success as a matter of ability, perserverance, and education (Berreman 1972; Warner *et al.* 1945).

In a castelike stratification people are, by contrast, assigned to their respective groups at birth or by ascribed criteria such as skin color, and they have few options to escape that designation. Each caste group (e.g., blacks in America) has its own class system but less opportunity for class differentiation and mobility than the dominant class system. For example, the job ceiling in the United States affects black-white racial stratification but not the stratification of social classes within the white group or within the black group. Caste thus gives class in the minority population added disadvantages: a white lower-class American is only lower class; a black lower-class American is also faced with a job ceiling and other caste barriers.

There is current debate over whether and to what extent class stratification has replaced racial or castelike stratification in America (Willie 1979; Wilson 1978). Since the 1960s, civil rights legislation and other efforts have raised the job ceiling and some-what reduced other racial barriers, but they have not eliminated these barriers altogether. No one knows the extent to which blacks are now employed in more desirable jobs as a matter of compliance with the law. What is certain is that the number of blacks in top jobs more than doubled after affirmative action leg-islation went into effect in 1966 and 1972; that there is a strong white resistance to these laws; and that blacks are still underre-presented in desirable jobs and overqualified for the jobs that they do (Brimmer 1974; U.S. Commission on Civil Rights 1978).

Furthermore, the positive changes have not reached far enough to affect significantly the social and economic conditions of the black lower class; nor have they been consistent through the years because of economic recessions, white backlash, and changes in political climate. Statistics easily conceal the single most important indication that castelike stratification persists in America: the extraordinary supports (affirmative action, Equal Employment Opportunities Commission Appeals, Special Pro-grams) that blacks need, but that whites do not, in order to move into the middle class. The pattern of change is significant for the problem of education and literacy in that black perceptions of American racial stratification and their opportunities within it have not grown to resemble the perceptions of the white popula-tion.

A Cultural Ecological Explanation of Black School Failure

The Framework

Cultural ecology provides a more adequate framework for under-standing the literacy problems of black and similar minorities, whether we focus on school completion, functional literacy, or performance on classroom and standardized tests. This frame-work enables us to study the connections between the school or learning processes *and* societal forces (such as economic patterns and opportunities, intergroup relations, and status mobility in a given society) which affect school curricula, classroom attitudes and efforts, and various activities of school personnel and other members of the educational system.

Cultural ecology is the study of institutionalized and socially transmitted patterns of behavior interdependent with features of the environment (Netting 1968:11; see also Geertz 1962; Goldschmidt 1971; Bennett 1969). It does not deal with the overall physical environment but with the effective environment, that is, those aspects that directly affect subsistence quest (techno-economic activities) and physical survival. In modern societies the effective environment is primarily the bureaucratized industrial economy. A given population's effective environment generally consists, however, of its resources, its ability to exploit these resources, and its level of technology. The principal economic activities or subsistence strategies depend upon the effective environment. And each mode of exploitation calls for specific skills, knowledge, and other attributes which facilitate subsistence and survival under the specific condition. Ecological adaptation for a given population consists of the congruence or fit between the population's strategies for subsistence, survival, and status and the instrumental competencies and related behaviors of its members. Adaptation for an individual consists of learning about resources and exploitative strategies and acquiring appropriate instrumental competencies and rules of behaviors for achievement as it is defined by for his or her social group.

Childrearing and formal education are culturally organized to insure that children in a given population meet these criteria for adaptation (Ogbu 1980). In modern societies the school is the principal institution adapting children to bureaucratized industrial economy in four ways: teaching them the basic practical skills of reading, writing, and computation essential for almost every subsistence activity in the economy; preparing them for more specialized job training when they later enter the labor force (Wilson 1973); socializing them by means of organizational features (teacher-pupil authority relations, the grading system, etc.) to develop social-emotional attributes essential for participation in the work force (Scrupski 1975; Wilcox 1978); and providing the credentials young adults need to enter the work force (Jencks 1972). In the latter role, schooling is more or less a culturally institutionalized device for allocating and rewarding individuals in society's status system, particularly in the economy (Ogbu 1979 a, b; 1980).

While ideologically most Americans do not see their schools this way, it is a reasonable analysis based on our own study of school and economic behaviors in Stockton, California. In our research, we asked people why they go to school; why they send their children to school; and why they pay taxes to support schools; we listened to public and private discussions and gossip about schooling, jobs, and related matters; we examined documents from local school systems and from city and county planning departments, as well as from employment and welfare agencies. These sources suggest that Stocktonians do not seek education for its own sake, to satisfy their curiosity, or for self-fulfillment, but in order to get jobs as adults and thereby achieve full adult status as defined by their community. Not only do Stocktonians believe that more and better schooling leads to more desirable jobs, higher income, and other social and economic benefits, but local statistics also tend to support their belief—for the majority whites: In Stockton, as elsewhere in the nation, whites with high school diplomas generally have a better chance at more desirable jobs and greater lifetime earning power than their peers with only elementary school diplomas; however they have less chance at desirable jobs and less earning power than their peers with college degrees.

The belief that economic opportunities are commensurate with educational achievement is a part of local white epistemology and is borne out historically by the actual experiences of most whites in the job market. The belief is communicated to local white children and reinforced in a variety of ways. These observations lead us to conclude that the school efforts of local whites are greatly influenced by their experiences in and perceptions of the connection between schooling and adult economic participation.

A major ecological consequence of castelike stratification and job ceiling is that blacks in Stockton and elsewhere in the United States have traditionally occupied economic positions characterized by scarce, dead-end, peripheral, or unstable jobs and by low wages, few chances for advancement on the job, and little social credit as measured by values of the larger society. Some ghetto blacks occupy economic positions that are almost devoid of any wage labor but that contain social resources such as other ghetto residents and caretaker institutions (Harrison 1972; Ross and Hill 1967). Equally important is the fact that the blacks' effective environment contains, in addition to these conventional resources, a subeconomy or "street economy" defined as "a market for the distribution of goods and services which are in demand but have

140

been outlawed officially for social and moral reasons (Bullock 1973: 100, see also Foster 1974; Heard 1968; Milner 1970; Wolfe 1970).

Educational Consequences

What are the educational consequences of the black effective environment? Because the traditional social and economic positions of blacks have not required much formal education or rewarded educational accomplishments highly, the pattern of schooling which has evolved for blacks generally prepares them for inferior roles. It does not qualify blacks for the more desirable social and economic positions open to whites, nor does it encourage blacks to achieve their maximum. These combined factors have traditionally affected black literacy as measured by school completion, functional literacy, and performance on classroom and standardized tests. We now want to suggest four specific ways in which these factors sustain the lag in black school performance by (a) promoting certain treatment or experiences of blacks in school and classroom and (b) fostering certain classroom attitudes, orientations, and behavior.

(1) White Perceptions of Blacks and Black Access to Education:

Blacks have had some access to formal schooling ever since they were brought to America in the early seventeenth century. Although formal education was available to only a few in the South (where most blacks lived before emancipation), and although there was strong opposition to black education in both the South and the North, actual legal prohibitions against black education were instituted in the South only from 1832 to about 1861 after Nat Turner's Revolt (Bond 1966:21; Bullock 1970). Black access to the public schools increased after emancipation, and, as the following table shows, their illiteracy rates steadily declined.

However, factors important to understanding the present situation are concealed by the table. First, blacks have had to fight for almost every increase in their access to public schools; in neither the South nor the North have they been free as a matter of right to attend their community public schools (Bond 1966; Bullock 1970; Kluger 1977; Ogbu 1978). Second, black education in both the South and North has usually been inferior, often separate, and generally based on white perceptions and stereotypes of black status in society and especially in the economy. Third, because blacks do not share white perceptions of their status, they tend not to accept white standards of education for them. Consequently, since the second half of the nineteenth century, blacks have been fighting whites against both inferior and separate education (Kluger 1977).

Let us briefly summarize how white perceptions of black status have shaped black education historically and affected the quality of black literacy.

Before emancipation, blacks received occasional biblical education because their masters believed it would make them more obedient and faithful. After the Civil War, when blacks were reiegated to peon-like status as sharecroppers or were limited to "Negro jobs" in domestic service and unskilled labor, education followed suit. The ruling white elites believed the tenant farming system would break down if black children received the same education as white children. They would, for example, learn to question the high rates of interest and the exploitative accounting methods the planters imposed on illiterate tenants. Thus, black education was starved of funds.

As the South urbanized, blacks at first received some "industrial" education, chiefly in cooking and low grade building skills. But when many desirable factory jobs began to require special training, black school curricula began, ironically, to emphasize classical and academic rather than industrial education, which was now offered in white schools (Bond 1966: 404, Myrdal 1944: 897–98; Ogbu 1978: 117).

We can conclude that, historically, if blacks did not qualify for desirable jobs it was because their education was designed to disqualify them, not because they were incompetent. Until perhaps the 1960s, American society never seriously intended blacks to achieve social and occupational equality with whites through education.

Even now, "subtle mechanisms" continue to adapt black and white graduates to different futures. One such mechanism for lowering the job ceiling is the disproportionate labeling of black children as educationally "handicapped." For example, in a recent court case brought by blacks against the San Francisco School District, evidence showed that blacks made up only 31.1 percent of the school enrollment in 1976–77, but constituted 53.8 percent of those categorized as educable mentally retarded and relegated to special classes. In the same year, in the twenty California school districts which enrolled 80 percent of black children, black students comprised about 27.5 percent of the school population but 62 percent of those labeled educable mentally retarded. In his decision favoring blacks the judge concluded that

Black and White Illiteracy, 14 Years Old and Over, by Region for Selected Years: 1890–1969

(Numbers in thousands)

Area and year	Black			White		
		Illiterate			Illiterate	
	Total	Number	Percent	Total	Number	Percent
United States:						
1890	4259	2607	61	35818	2880	8
1910	823	91	11	43091	1944	5
1930	8027	1445	18	77357	2350	3
1947	10471	1152	11	95952	1919	2
1959	12210	910	7	109163	1709	2
1969	14280	509	4	127449	891	1
South:						
1890	3769	2462	65	7755	1170	15
1910	5308	1906	36	12790	1087	8
1930	6116	1351	22	18390	780	4
North and West:						
1890	631	208	33	28063	1710	6
1910	823	91	11	43091	1944	5
1930	1911	94	5	58967	1570	3

Source: U.S. Department of Commerce, Bureau of the Census. *Current Population Reports, Special Studies, Series P-23, No. 80, The Social and Economic Status of the Black Population in the United States: An Historical View, 1790–1978.* Table 68, p. 91.

> The statistical analyses of the statewide and district-by-district figures indicate the obvious. Their (i.e., black) apparent overenrollment could not be the result of chance. For example, there is less than one in a million chance that the overenrollment of black children and the underenrollment of non-black children in the E.M.R. classes in 1976–77 would have resulted under a color-blind system of placement (U.S. District Court for Northern California, 1979: 21–22).

The figures are similar to those of other large American cities, including Chicago and New York (see, for example, U.S. Commission on Civil Rights, 1974).

(2) *Black Responses*

We pointed out earlier that castelike minorities do not usually accept their subordination passively and that blacks have been fighting since emancipation for more and better schooling and against the job ceiling. Those responses, as they relate to schooling and jobs, may in fact contribute to the lag in the school performance, as we shall demonstrate.

A. *Black School Conflict and Mistrust:* History has left blacks with a feeling that whites and their institutions cannot be trusted to benefit blacks equitably. Public schools, particularly in the ghetto, are generally not trusted by blacks to provide black children with the "right education." This mistrust of schools arises partly from black perceptions of past and current discriminatory treatment by public schools. This treatment is fully documented in several studies (see Bond 1966, 1969; Kluger 1977; Weinberg 1977).

For over a century, having first "fought" against total exclusion from the public schools, blacks have been "fighting" against inferior education in both segregated and integrated schools. In the totally segregated Southern school systems, blacks of course identified strongly and therefore cooperated with "black schools." But their effectiveness was undermined by their simultaneous rejection of these same schools as inferior to white schools and thus their need to "fight" for school desegregation. Their attention, commitment, and efforts were diverted from maximizing achievement in black schools to the pursuit of equal resources and an ideal learning setting, namely, desegregated schools.

But in desegregated schools throughout the nation disaffection and mistrust also abound because blacks see inferior education perpetuated through many subtle devices they suspected the schools of using (e.g., biased testing, misclassification, tracking, biased textbooks, biased counseling, etc.), and because they doubt that these schools understand black children and their needs.

This doubt is particularly widespread at the moment: it was openly expressed by many blacks at public meetings and in ethnographic interviews during our fieldwork in Stockton. In a study of a desegregated high school, Scherer and Slawski (1977) also found that local blacks tended to attribute low school performance of black males to the school's inability to "relate to black males in ways that will help them learn." The point we would like to stress is that black mistrust and conflict with schools reduce the degree to which black parents and their children can accept as legitimate the schools' goals, standards, and instructional approaches. As a result they tend not to experience a need to cooperate with the schools or to follow their rules and requirements for achievement.

The same conflicts and mistrust also force the schools into defensive approaches to black education—control, paternalism, or actual "contests"—which divert the attention of both blacks and schools from the real task of educating black children. This contrasts sharply with the experience of white middle-class parents and their children, who tend to see the completion of school tasks and conformity with school standards as necessary, desirable, and compatible with their own goals. Ghetto blacks tend sometimes to interpret the same demands as deceptions or as unnecessary impositions incompatible with their "real educational goals." Perseverance at academic tasks thus becomes difficult for black children.

B. *Disillusionment Over Job Ceiling and Academic Efforts:* Throughout history a greater proportion of blacks than whites have been educationally better qualified or overqualifed for their jobs yet underpaid for their educational achievements (Henderson 1967; Norgren and Hill 1967; Newman *et al* 1978; Sharp 1970; U.S. Commission on Civil Rights 1978). Even in recent years their gradual penetration into more desirable jobs has been accomplished mainly through collective struggle for civil rights (Newman *et al* 1978; Scott 1976; Ogbu 1978). Job opportunities remain the primary concern of black Americans today.

The job ceiling and related discriminatory practices shape black operations, which in turn influence their perceptions of and responses to schooling. Blacks are generally bitter, frustrated, and resentful at the job ceiling and other barriers to the full benefits of their education. The extent of this bitterness is evident in the time and resources they expend in efforts to break or circumvent the job ceiling (see Davis, Gardner and Gardner

145

1965; Dollard 1957; Drake and Cayton 1970; Ogbu 1974; Powdermaker 1968; Newman *et al* 1978; Scott 1976) as are their strategies for achieving their objectives, such as "uncle tomming," boycotting white businesses, protesting, rioting, and appealing to the courts, to Fair Employment Practices Commissions, to the Equal Employment Opportunity Commission, and the like (see Drake and Cayton 1970:745; National Advisory Commission on Civil Disorders, *Report* 1968:61; Newman *et al* 1978:10–26; Ogbu 1978; Powdermaker 1968:107, 100, 112; Schemer 1965:85).

When civil rights effectively expand black employment opportunities and other rewards for education, as they appeared to be doing in the 1960s, this encourages black students to work hard in school (Ginsberg et al 1967). But a discouraging message is also communicated, namely, that without such a collective civil rights struggle, blacks automatically have fewer opportunities than whites to benefit from education.

Black children learn about the job ceiling and other barriers quite early in life, though not necessarily from explicit statements by their parents and other adults in their community. In our ethnographic research in Stockton, California, we have found, however, that black parents communicate contradictory attitudes toward schooling. They emphasize the need for their children to get more education than they did, and they insist that their children work hard in order to get good grades and to graduate from high school or college. However, the same parents, by being unemployed, underemployed, and discriminated against, and by gossiping about the similar experiences of relatives and other adults in the community, imply that even if the children succeed in school their chances at good jobs and other societal rewards are not as good as those of their white peers. It is also a part of local black epistemology that a black person must be "twice as good" or "twice as qualified" as the white in order to compete successfully in any situation where whites are judges. Thus the actual example of the lives of black parents can undercut their stated encouragements.

Black children also learn about the job ceiling from public demonstrations calling for more jobs and better wages and from mass media reports of these and related events. These sources convey to black children that the connection between school success and one's ability to get ahead is not as good for blacks as for whites. As black children get older and experience personal failures and frustrations in looking for part-time jobs and summer jobs, these negative messages are reinforced. Some perceptions of young blacks, such as their impression of unlimited employment opportunities for their white peers, may not be accurate (Ogbu 1974); they nonetheless lead to increasing disillusionment among blacks about their future and to doubts about the value of schooling (Ogbu 1974:100; see also Frazier 1940:134–47; Schulz 1969:159; Powdermaker 1968:321).

Not only do these perceptions discourage black children from developing serious attitudes toward school and from persevering in their schoolwork; they also teach them to "blame the system" rather than themselves for their failures. In our research in Stockton we have found that black children learn very early to blame the school system for their failures, just as their parents and black adults in general blame their failures on the larger "system." A resulting paradox is that black students may express high educational aspirations coupled with low academic effort and perseverance and thus low school performance.

C. *Survival Strategies and Competencies Incongruent with Demands of Schooling:* Another black response to the job ceiling is the evolution of "survival strategies." This effects even children much too young to understand the labor market and other barriers and has serious implications for school performance and classroom processes. There are two kinds of survival strategies. The purpose of the first kind is to increase conventional economic and social resources of the black community and to make available conventional jobs and other societal rewards. These strategies include collective struggles or civil rights activities (Newman *et al* 1978; Scott 1976), clientship or uncle tomming (Dollard 1957; Myrdal 1944; Farmer 1968; Ogbu 1978). Civil rights strategy is well known to most people; but clientship also arises from the job ceiling and other barriers. Blacks learned long ago that one key to self-betterment within the caste system is through white patronage (i.e., favoritism, not merit alone), which can be solicited through some version of the old "Uncle Tom" role, that is, through compliance, dependence, and manipulation. More recently the reverse strategy of "shuckin' and jivin'" has been adopted, which is another defensive way to manipulate white patronage. The second kind of survival strategy, which includes hustling, pimping, and the like, exploits nonconventional economic and social resources or "the street economy" (Bullock 1973; Foster 1974; Heard 1968; Milner 1970; Wolfe 1970).

Thus within the black community success in terms of conventional jobs and resources often requires collective struggles and/or clientship *in addition to educational credentials.* Nonconventional forms of success and ways of making a living are also open to blacks. Thus "successful people" are not only those who suc-

147

ceed in conventional terms either with school credentials alone or with clientship and collective struggle as well, but also those who make it in the street through hustling and related strategies. They are admired, and they influence the efforts of others, including children, to succeed.

We have suggested that survival strategies may require knowledge, attitudes, and skills that are not wholly compatible with white middle-class teaching and learning behavior. We have also suggested that children learn the survival strategies during preschool years as a normal part of their cultural learning; consequently, the potential for learning difficulties may already exist when children enter school. Whether and to what extent those difficulties arise depends on the individual child's experience in school and the classroom. We suspect that insofar as children have become competent in these survival strategies they may lack serious attitudes toward school and toward academic tasks in general, including test taking.

Conclusion

In this paper we have argued that the disproportionate school failure of black children is not because they come from an oral culture, though we have not challenged the assertion that black culture is an oral culture. We have only noted that members of the so-called oral cultures of small-scale societies and immigrants into the United States from residual cultures of more complex societies do not manifest the same learning problems in school that are found among black and similar castelike minorities.

We have suggested an alternative view of the problem within an ecological framework in which schooling is a culturally organized means of preparing children for adult roles in the social and economic life of their society or social group. Within this framework the traditional social and economic positions of blacks have not required much education nor rewarded blacks highly for educational accomplishments. Black menial positions enforced by castelike or racial stratification has influenced how the dominant whites who control their schooling perceive them and define their educational needs. It has also influenced how blacks themselves perceive their opportunities and the importance of schooling.

The perceptions of whites have led them to provide blacks with inadequate schooling and to communicate attitudes in school settings that do not encourage blacks to maximum efforts.

Black perceptions generate disillusionment about schooling and a lack of perseverance toward schoolwork; they lead to survival strategies that require knowledge, attitudes, and skills which may be incompatible with school requirements. Furthermore, it is likely that perennial conflict and mistrust between blacks and the schools interfere with the willingness of blacks to comply with school rules and standards and place the schools in a defensive posture toward blacks. Closer study is needed to determine how these factors contribute, singly and in combination, to the learning difficulties observed in classrooms.

Since the 1960s some efforts have been made to change black status and schooling, for example, through legislative and administrative channels noted earlier in the essay. The magnitude and quality of these changes, however, have not broken the job ceiling or significantly altered black expectations, especially among the lower segments of the black community.

During the same period, efforts have also been made to improve black schooling and raise academic achievement levels through school desegregation, compensatory education, preschool (Headstart) educations, parent education and training, Follow-Through, special admissions, special scholarships, and many others (Ogbu 1978). These programs have helped many blacks to complete higher levels of schooling, to achieve greater functional literacy, and to improve their performance in classroom and on standardized tests. But the number benefiting from such programs remains small and many who do benefit probably do not come from the lower segments of the community. These programs remain ineffective for or unavailable to the majority. Moreover, they are essentially remedial and often based on misconceptions of the underlying causes of black school problems (Ogbu 1978). Preventing learning problems before they develop will require a strategy that will simultaneously have to (a) consider the economic expectations of blacks as a root cause rather than a consequence of the school failure and literacy problem; (b) eliminate the gross and subtle mechanisms which differentiate black schooling from white schooling; and (c) examine black perceptions and "adaptive" responses, including the problem of mistrust and conflict in black relations with the schools.

Bibliography

Abrahams, Roger D.
   1970 "The Training of the Man of Words in Talking Sweet." *Language and Society*, 1:15–29.
Baratz, Joan

1969 "Teaching Reading in an Urban Negro School System." In J. Baratz and Roger Shuy, eds, *Teaching Black Children to Read*. Washington, D.C.: Center for Applied Linguistics, pp. 92–116.

Bennett, John W.

1969 *Northern Plainsmen: Adaptative Strategy and Agricultural Life*. Arlington Heights, Ill: AHM Pub.

Berreman, Gerald D.

1972 "Race, Caste, and Other Invidious Distinctions in Social Stratification." *Race*, 24(4).

Bond, Horace Mann

1966 *The Education of the Negro in the American Social Order*. New York: Octagon Books, Inc.

1969 *Negro Education in Alabama: A Study in Cotton and Steel*. New York: Atheneum.

Brimmer, Andrew F.

1974 "Economic Development in the Black Community." In Eli Ginsberg and Robert M. Solow, eds. *The Great Society: Lessons for the Future*. New York: Basic Books, pp. 146–63.

Bullock, Henry Allen

1970 *A History of Negro Education in the South: From 1619 to the Present*. New York: Praeger.

Bullock, Paul

1973 *Aspiration vs. Opportunity: "Careers" In the Inner City*. Ann Arbor: Michigan University Press.

Cole, Michael, and Sylvia Scribner

1973 "Cognitive Consequences of Formal and Informal Education." *Science*, 182: 553–59.

Cook-Gumperz, Jenny, and John J. Gumperz

1979 "From Oral To Written Culture: The Transition To Literacy." In Marcia Farr Whitehead, ed. *Variation in Writing*. New York: Erlbaum Associates, in press.

Davis, Allison, Burleigh B. and Mary R. Gardner

1965 *Deep South: A Social Anthropological Study of Caste and Class*. Abridged Edition. Chicago: The University of Chicago Press.

Dollard, John

1957 *Caste and Class in a Southern Town*, 3rd ed. Garden City: Doubleday Anchor Books.

Drake, St. Claire, and Horace Cayton

1970 *Black Metropolis: A Study of Negro Life in a Northern City*. New York: Harcourt, Brace, & World. 2 vols.

Erickson, Frederick

1978 *Mere Ethnography: Some Problems in Its Use in Educational Practice*. Past Presidential Address Delivered at the Annual Meeting of the Council on Anthropology and Education, Los Angeles Calif. Nov. 1978.

Erickson, Frederick, and J. Mohatt

1977 *The Social Organization of Participant Structure in Two Classrooms of Indian Students*. Unp. Ms.

Farmer, James

1968 "Stereotypes of the Negro and Their Relationship to His Self-Image." In Herbert C. Rudman and Richard L. Fetherstone, eds. *Urban Schooling*. New York: Harcourt, Brace, & World.

Foster, Herbert L.

1974, *Ribbin', Jivin', and Playin' the Dozens: The Unrecognized Dilemma of Inner City Schools.* Cambridge, Mass: Ballinger.

Frazier, E. Franklin
1940 *Negro Youth at the Crossways: Their Personality Development in the Middle States.* Washington, D.C.: American Council on Education.

Geertz, Clifford
1962 *Agricultural Involution: The process of Ecological Change in Indonesia,* Berkeley: University of California Press.

Ginzberg, Eli, et al.
1967 *The Middle-Class Negro in the White Man's World.* New York: Columbia University Press.

Goldschmidt, Walter
1971 "Introduction: The Theory of Cultural Adaptation." In Robert B. Edgerton, *The Individual In Cultural Adaptation: A Study of Four East African Peoples.* Berkeley: University of California Press, pp. 1–22.

Goody, Jack
1977 *The Domestication of the Savage Mind.* Cambridge: Cambridge University Press.

Greenfield, Patricia M.
1966 "On Culture and Conservation." In Jerome S. Bruner, et al., eds. *Studies in Cognitive Growth.* New York: Wiley, p. 225–56.

Gumperz, John J.
1980 "Conversational Inferences and Classroom Learning." In Judith Green and Cynthia Wallat, eds. *Ethnographic Approaches to Face-to-Face Interaction.* Ablex Pub. Co., in press.

Gumperz, John J., and Jenny Cook-Gumperz
1979 *Beyond Ethnography: Some Uses of Sociolinguistics for Understanding Classroom Environments.* A Paper Presented at the AERA Conference, San Francisco, April 1979.

Harrison, Bennett
1972 *Education, Training and the Urban Ghetto.* Baltimore Md.: The Johns Hopkins University Press.

Heard, N. C.
1968 *Howard Street.* New York: Dial Press.

Henderson, Vivian W.
1967 "Regions, Race and Jobs." In Arthur M. Ross and Herbert Hill, eds. *Employment, Race and Poverty.* New York: Harcourt, Brace, & World. pp. 76–104.

Heyneman, Stephen P.
1979 "Why Impoverished Children Do Well in Ugandan Schools." *Comparative Education,* 15:175–85.

Jencks, Christopher
1972 *Inequality.* New York: Basic Books.

Koehler, Virginia
1978 "Classroom Process Research: Present and Future." *The Journal of Classroom Interaction,* 13:3–11.

Kochman, Thomas
1973 "Orality and Literacy as Factors in 'Black' and 'White' Communicative Behavior." *International Journal of the Sociology of Language,* pp. 91–115.

Kluger, Richard
1977 *Simple Justice.* New York: Vintage Books.

Labov, William

1972 *Language in the Inner City*. Philadelphia: University of Pennsylvania Press.

1969 "The Logic of Nonstandard English." *Georgetown University Monographs in Language and Linguistics*, 72: 1–31.

Lewis, Diane K.

1979 *Schooling, Literacy and Sense Modality*. Unp. Ms., U.S. Santa Cruz.

Luria, A. R.

1976 *Cognitive Development: Its Cultural and Social Foundations*. Cambridge, Mass.: Harvard University Press.

Milner, Christina Andrea

1970 *Black Pimps and Their Prostitutes*. Ph.D. Dissertation, Department of Anthropology, University of California, Berkeley.

Myrdal, Gunnar

1944 *An American Dilemma*. New York: Harper. vol. 2.

The National Advisory Commission on Civil Disorders

1968 *Report*. Washington, D.C.: U.S. Government Printing Office.

Newman, Dorothy K., et al.

1978 *Protest, Politics, and Prosperity: Black Americans and White Institutions, 1940–1975*. New York: Pantheon Books.

Norgren, Paul H., and Samuel E. Hill

1964 *Toward Fair Employment*, New York: Columbia University Press.

Netting, Robert McC

1968 *Hill Farmers of Nigeria*. Seattle: University of Washington Press.

Ogbu, John U.

1980a *An Ecological Approach to Minority Education*, Unp. Ms. 1980b *Ethnoecology of Urban Schooling*. Unp. Ms.

1979 *Origins of Human Competence: A Cultural Ecological Perspective*. Unp. Ms.

1978 *Minority Education and Caste: The American System in Crosscultural Perspective*. New York: Academic Press.

1974 *The Next Generation: An Ethnography of Education in an Urban Neighborhood*. New York: Academic Press.

Pepper, Suzanne

1971 "Education and Political Development in Communist China." *Studies in Comparative Communism*, 3 (3&4).

Philips, Susan U.

1972 "Participant Structure and Communicative Competence: Warm Springs Children in Community and Classrooms." In Courtney B. Cazden, Vera P. John and Dell Hymes, eds. *Functions of Language in the Classroom*. New York: Teachers College Press.

Powdermaker, Hortense

1968 *After Freedom*. New York: Atheneum.

Rentel, V., and J. Kennedy

1972 "Effects of Pattern Drill on the Phonology, Syntax, and Reading Achievement of Rural Appalachian Children." *American Educational Research Journal*, 9:87–100.

Ross, Arthur M., and Herbert Hill, eds.

1967 *Employment, Race and Poverty*. New York: Harcourt, Brace & World.

Schemer, George

1965 "Effectiveness of Equal Opportunity Legislation." Herbert N. Northrup and Richard L. Rowan, eds. *The Negro Employment Opportunity*. Ann Arbor: University of Michigan Press, pp. 67–107.

Schulz, David A.

1969 *Coming Up Black*. Englewood, Cliffs, N.J.: Prentice-Hall.

Scott, Joseph W.
1976 *The Black Revolt.* Cambridge, Mass.: Schenkman.
Scrupski, Adam
1975 "The Social System of the School." In Kenneth Shimahara and Adam Scrupski, eds. *Social Forces and Schooling.* New York: McKay.
Sharp, Laure M.
1970 *Education and Employment.* Baltimore, Md.: Johns Hopkins Univ. Press.
Simons, Herbert D.
1976 *Black Dialect, Reading Interference and Classroom Interaction.* Dept. of Education, University of California, Berkeley. Unp. Ms.
Slawski, Edward J., and Jacqueline Scherer
1977 "The Rhetoric of Concern—Trust and Control in an Urban Desegregated School." *Anthropology and Education Quarterly* 9 (1)
Snow, Edgar
1961 *Red Star Over China.* New York: Grove Press, Inc.
Stewart, William A.
1969 "On the Use of Negro Dialect in the Teaching of Reading." In Joan Baratz and Roger Shuy, eds. *Teaching Black Children to Read.* Washington, D.C.: Center for Applied Linguistics, pp. 156–219.
U.S. Commission on Civil Rights
1978 *Social Indicators of Equality for Minorities and Women.* Washington, D.C.: U.S. Government Printing Office.
1974 *Bilingual/Bicultural Education: A Privilege or a Right?* Washington, D.C.: U.S. Government Printing Office.
U.S. Department of Commerce, Bureau of the Census
1979 *The Social and Economic Status of the Black Population in the United States: An Historical View, 1790–1969. Special Studies, Series P-23, No. 80.* Washington, D.C.: U.S. Government Printing Office.
U.S. District Court for Northern California
1979 *Opinion: Larry P. vs. Riles.* San Francisco, California.
van der Berghe, Pierre
1979 "Review: *Minority Education and Caste.*" *Comparative Education Review,* forthcoming.
Warner, W. Lloyd, et al.
1945 *Who Shall Be Educated?* New York. Harper.
Weiberg, Meyer
1977 *A Chance To Learn: A History of Race and Education in the United States.* New York: Cambridge University Press.
Wilcox, Kathleen
1978 *Schooling and Socialization for Work Roles.* Ph. D. Dissertation, Dept. of Anthropology, Harvard University.
Willie, Charles Vert, ed.
1979 *Caste and Class Controversy.* New York: Green Hall, Inc.
Wilson, H. Clyde
1973 "On the Evolution of Education." In Solon T. Kimball and Jacquetta-Hill Burnett, eds. *Learning and Culture.* Seattle: University of Washington Press, pp. 211–41.
Wilson, William Julius
1978 *The Declining Significance of Race.* Chicago: University of Chicago Press.
Wolfe, Tom
1970 *Radical Chic and Mau-Mauing the Flack Catchers.* New York: Strauss and Giroux.

Readings on Literacy:
A Bibliographical Essay

by Tela Zasloff

Tela Zasloff is a doctoral candidate in the rhetoric program at Carnegie-Mellon University and has an M.A. in English literature from the University of California, Berkeley. She has held a number of research and editing positions. Her current interest is in research on writing.

In this essay we will look at literacy as it ranges over various fields that are not represented directly in this volume but which have influenced the thinking of its contributors. Most of our attention will focus on cognitive anthropology, social psychology, and sociolinguistics, but we will also consider contributions from philosophy, religion, rhetoric, and developmental economics.

The following sample of books and articles from these fields articulates the concerns of distinct disciplines and the direction of research in progress. No matter what the authors' special concerns about literacy, they concur on its cultural significance: the manner in which social groups rely on written language reflects and modifies the structure of their thought processes, the nature of their self-expression, and their dialogue with others. A pervasive theme of the works under review here is that we must keep challenging our own assumptions about written language if we hope to understand ourselves and our communication with others.

The Oral Tradition

Many students of literacy speculate about the consequences of moving from oral to written modes. They have asked whether the introduction of writing does not bring a sense of alienation from society, a stratification of concepts and values, and a loss of ability to memorize and remember. This section covers a half-dozen articles and books by leading scholars concerned with the oral tradition and its legacy.

155

One of the most stimulating articles on this topic is "The Consequences of Literacy" by Jack Goody and Ian Watt.[1] Speaking from the viewpoint of cultural anthropology, Goody and Watt argue that the invention of writing, produced by the urban revolution of the Ancient Near East, changed the whole structure of human culture. The full-fledged system of writing which emerged from the Greek world of the seventh century B.C. provided permanently recorded versions of the past and encouraged the development of historical inquiry and a skepticism about the mythical cosmologies. At the same time, such a writing system made possible and testable alternative explanations about the universe and the development of logic, specialized learning, and a cumulative intellectual tradition.

The contribution of literacy to our culture, however, has been marked by tensions. The authors point out the problematic role of literacy in several areas, among them political democracy, cultural integration, and expressive action. The ease of alphabetic reading and writing was important to the development of political democracy, although writing, paradoxically, by illuminating the differences between past and present and the inconsistencies in cultural tradition, has made consensus and cohesion less possible. In a similar vein, they note the impossibility of fully assimilating the knowledge of a literate culture compared with the assimilation possible in an oral culture. This means that in the literate culture the individual strives to acquire new knowledge while at the same time feeling alienated from the past. (The authors quote Nietzsche at this point: "We moderns are wandering encyclopedias . . . obsessed by an historical sense that injures and finally destroys.")

Writing also leads to social stratifications in modern societies based on how well men handle their tools of writing and reading. Modern education creates discontinuities between the public literate culture of the school and the private oral culture of the family. The social tension produced between such oral and literate orientations in the West is paralleled by an intellectual one, which leads to a nostalgia for myth—as seen in Plato, Rousseau, Cervantes, and Tolstoy. Moreover, the technique of writing itself results in an individualization of personal experience, encourages private thought, and increases awareness of individual differences. Nonetheless, radio, movies, and television counterbalance the individualization of reading and writing and allow the kind of direct personal interaction with experience that was possible through oral tradition.

David Olson, in "From Utterance to Text"[2] argues on the same basis as Goody and Watt that there is a transition from utterance to text that is characterized by an increasing explicitness and autonomy of language meaning. After reviewing some major theories of language acquisition, Olson traces the history of text, beginning with Greek literacy and reaching "its most visible form" in the British essayists. In his view, analytical writing, developed by the Greeks, increased the explicitness of language. Analytic writing does this by minimizing the number of possible interpretations of a statement by construction of sentences in which meaning is dictated by syntactic and lexical elements. He concludes by noting three major differences between utterances and texts. In regard to meaning, utterances appeal to shared experiences, interpretations, and intuition; texts appeal to rules of logic for implications and are formal rather than intuitive. Where truth is concerned, the oral tradition sees truth as wisdom, while the text sees truth as simply correspondence, in the disinterested province of the scientist. Concerning functions, utterance is interpersonal and rhetorical, while written text remains logical and ideational.

These hypotheses have been tested by others in field studies. In "Oral and Written Language," Patricia Greenfield[3] compares the effects of oral and written traditions on specific cultural groups in Africa, the United States, and England. She characterizes oral language speakers as relying more on context for communication, which results from the fact that communication is most often face to face in oral cultures and shared by smaller groups. In this kind of culture, the teaching of skills has a contextual nature in which teaching is conducted through demonstration, as with basket weaving. Studies show, Greenfield further claims, that "a context-dependent teaching style on the part of most mothers is associated with a lesser development of ability to form conceptual and linguistic abstractions on the part of the child." Some of the most successful educational programs for lower class children, she continues, focus on developing context-independent communication.

The results of her study have led her to the hypothesis that school teaches a grouping of operations generated by the nature of the written language. Because writing uses linguistic contexts independently of immediate reference, it clears the way for symbolic manipulation and Piaget's stage of formal operations. She concludes that context-dependent forms of speech and thought are more primitive than context-free ones. Because we have both language habits in a written culture, it is important for meaningful human communication that the two be used interchangeably and flexibly as the situation demands.

The revival of the thought modes of the oral tradition through new electronic technologies is a central theme in the writings of Marshall McLuhan. *The Gutenberg Galaxy,*[4] he tells his readers, "is intended to trace the ways in which the *forms* of experience and of mental outlook and expression have been modified by modes of communication." Comparing our era with the Elizabethan "typographical" age, McLuhan sees both ages facing a similar problem of cultural change—we are "confronting an electric technology which would seem to render individualism obsolete" just as the Elizabethans were confronting individualism, which seemed to have brought into obsolescence the "medieval corporate experience." Our age, the author concludes, is under a strain as the older patterns of perception encounter new structures. These older patterns are based in Cartesian logic, presenting the universe as an immense mechanism which can be described by localization of its parts in space and over time. In our new electric age of the past 150 years, our technological instruments reformed our perceptive apparatus by extending our senses simultaneously and globally, so that our consciousness has become collective, our thought processes, dynamic. Thus, to McLuhan, the electric age returns us to the oral tradition, recreating "this world in the image of a global village."

Father Walter Ong, studying the evolution of modern consciousness in *Interfaces of the Word,*[5] shares McLuhan's view that writing has generated alienation in human life. It has restructured consciousness "creating new interior distances within the psyche." His book is a collection of essays on this theme, dealing with psychic distances between writers and audience; the tendency of print to set up "closed-off economies of thought and utterance"; and new modes of thought associated with television and with the ecology movements.

Ortega Y Gasset discusses one of Ong's themes—the distance between writer and reader—in "The Difficulty of Reading,"[6] a paper prepared for a university seminar on Plato. He asserts that "to read" implies understanding a text fully, but this is impossible and utopian since we always read our own interpretations into a text. Reading, then, is an active construction of all the reality which is not expressed in the text, but which is indispensable for a more satisfactory understanding. From this view he develops two axioms: every utterance is deficient, saying less than it wishes to; every utterance is exuberant, saying more than it plans.

To accomplish interpretation, we must understand the conditions under which a text is written. These conditions explain why reading is a problematical operation: (1) it is always limited "by a frontier of ineffability—that which cannot be said in any language"; (2) it is limited by the kinds of information that every language passes over in silence, that the hearer is expected to add from the context; (3) as speech, it not only has to include articulation but also to imply gesture, modulation of voice, and posture.

Because a book, a text, is entirely verbal and nothing more, disconnected from bodily expression, the book is equivocal and ambiguous in its entirety. This was Plato's view of texts. In the *Phaedrus,* books are considered to contain dead language and expression. Yet paradoxically, Plato is the first author who wrote books on a gigantic scale, because the relative impersonality of the written word gives the expression a distance and objectivity which are indispensable for transmitting theories.

Cultural Differences and Instruction

The authors in this section, from the fields of sociolinguistics, psychology, and rhetoric, look at the relationship between oral tradition, cultural differences, and instructional goals. Basil Bernstein in "Social Class and Linguistic Development" [7] argues that speech marks out distinct types of relationships with the social environment. Certain forms of language use are strategic for educational and occupational success, and these forms are culturally determined. He characterizes the language use of the working-class child as maximizing "the direct experience of affective inclusiveness rather than verbally conditioned emotional and cognitive differentiation." In this type of language use, the sentences are short and grammatically simple, there is little use of subordinate clauses, there is an inability to hold a formal subject through a speech sequence, an infrequent use of categoric statements, an infrequent use of impersonal pronouns, a large number of reinforcing phrases and idiomatic sequences, and a general language of implicit meaning.

This "public language" emphasizes the importance of social relationships at the cost of the formal, logical structure of communication. As the moral implications of his theory, Bernstein argues that if public language symbolizes tradition and important social relationships to a child, to simply substitute a formal language is to cut him off from his roots and perhaps alienate him.

The author suggests that changing a linguistic system may require modifying the social structure itself.

Doris Entwisle,[8] in "Implications of Language Socialization for Reading Models and for Learning to Read," makes some extensions from Bernstein's theory. She suggests that in learning to read, social and ethnic groups have large differences in cognitive style, including what is attended to and the approach to problems. She sees two major implications for reading research: a need for explicit recognition of group differences; a need for explicit recognition of social contexts in reading. Specifically, she views the following as research needs: (1) separating out modes of speech among groups from other variables such as IQ; (2) investigation of data from bilingual experiments which suggest that social factors dwarf linguistic ones in second-language learning; (3) tests of Bernstein's basic assumption relating social contexts of language use to educability.

In *The Cultural Context of Learning and Thinking*, Cole, Gay, Glick, and Sharp[9] ask some of the same basic questions as Bernstein and Entwisle. What are the sources of cultural differences in language use and ability? What is the meaning of those differences? George Miller introduces the volume as a test of a myth long existent in anthropological and psychological theory: that nonliterate people have a primitive, inferior mentality that is highly concrete, illogical, and insensitive to contradictions, and that the primitive mind is childish and emotional when compared to modern Western maturity and logical consistency. The authors argue that it is culture that develops the cognitive processes and that, rather than applying tests developed in Western contexts to primitive people, we should be testing them on things for which their experience has prepared them, to discover what cognitive strategies they are using.

The study grew out of an attempt to determine why Liberian tribal children have great difficulty with Western-style mathematics. The authors found that there were certain tasks that these children did better than Americans (e.g., estimating various amounts of rice) and certain ones which gave them more trouble (e.g., measuring lengths). The source of the differences between these two kinds of tasks related directly to the demands of rice farming, which is central to the tribal culture. The theory implicit in this is that primitive cultures make different kinds of intellectual demands than do technologically advanced ones and that skills in cognition are therefore culture specific. By looking at the Kpelle tribe, the authors sought, in the cultural environment, explanations of the fact that different groups manifest different intellectual behaviors.

In their concluding chapter, the authors suggest that their approach can be applied to the problem of subcultural differences in cognitive behavior in the United States, particularly their major conclusion that "cultural differences in cognition reside more in the situations to which particular cognitive processes are applied than in the existence of a process in one particular culture group and its absence in another." The task for the future is to determine the conditions through which cognitive processes are revealed and to develop techniques for establishing these conditions in the appropriate educational setting.

The next three authors focus on pedagogic theories for reading and writing. In *Learning to Read,* Jeanne Chall[10] points out that for over a decade there has been a debate about every basic issue in beginning reading, with challenges from laymen, popular writers, college English teachers, linguists, sociologists, and psychologists. By bringing together the relevant facts of this debate, Chall wants to determine if changes in the practice of teaching beginning reading are justified by existing evidence and why the changes were proposed in the first place. The study reveals that research results are only one of the factors influencing beginning reading instruction, some of the others being publishing houses, schools of education, parents' meetings, and classroom environments.

Chall makes five major recommendations: (1) The phonetic code-emphasis method—learning the printed code for the spoken language—produces better results in comprehension and the mechanical aspects of reading up to the end of third grade and should be used; the easiest way to initiate a modification in method is to change the instructional materials for children and the teachers' manuals. (2) Current ideas about content in basal readers should be reexamined; Chall's personal preference is folktales and fairy tales which have universal appeal, especially because of their emotional content. (3) Grade levels should be reevaluated and vocabularies increased in basal readers. (4) New standardized tests should be developed which examine both individual components of the reading process and mastery of reading over a time period. (5) Reading research must be improved so that findings can be organized in computerized storage and retrieval services, research can be coordinated to save duplication, and research can be guided by the norms of science.

Elsasser and John-Steiner raise the question of how composition skills can best be developed in "An Interactionist Approach to Advancing Literacy."[11] They draw on the work of Paulo Freire and Lev Vygotsky in connecting writing to certain cognitive states and social conditions. From Vygotsky they have adopted the concept of writing as multiple transformations of "inner speech" (which originated in social interaction) to an abstract, maximally detailed mode requiring deliberate semantics. Mastery of this transformation depends on cognitive processes and the social context in which the writing is produced. Vygotsky makes the proposition that words are shaped both by the individual consciousness and by the collective, sociohistorical experience, so that only people touched by social transformations and convinced they can shape their social reality can participate in a dialogue with the outer world and feel a need for educationally transmitted knowledge. Particularly in poor and Third World countries, educational intervention without actual social change is ineffective.

The authors present, as a teaching method, a pilot program for teaching writing in New Mexico, designed according to an "intricate interaction" among teachers, learners, and factors of social change. They support exercises on elaborating a scene so that others can identify it, asking others to reproduce a geometric design according to one student's directions, and tapping the abbreviated nature of inner speech. The principal questions behind these exercises include: What is shared knowledge? What are the information needs of the audience? What are the particularities of the writer's experience? What are the linguistic prejudices of the audience?

In the field of rhetoric, one of the major concerns has been the teaching of written composition in secondary schools, colleges, and universities. During the past fifteen to twenty years, rhetorical theory has focused on the process of writing itself, including the generation of ideas in composition and the question of how to teach this process. In *Rhetoric: Discovery and Change,* Young, Becker, and Pike[12] address this question of teaching the discovery of ideas—or "invention," as it is known in classical rhetorical theory. They argue that any grammatical unit is part of a whole hierarchical pattern of language in which small units are parts of larger ones, and this grammatical hierarchy, in turn, is part of a larger system of language which includes a lexical hierarch (words) and a phonological one (sounds, letters, and punctuation). These language systems symbolize the whole hierarchical system by which we perceive experience and thus permit choice, patterning, and manipulation on the part of the writer.

If any experience, including language, is perceived as occurring in repeatable patterns, the authors maintain, then we should be able to understand an experience by analyzing its patterns from three possible points of view: (1) its contrastive features; (2) its range of variations; (3) its distribution in larger contexts. Applying these three basic viewpoints to the writing process, the authors present a large number of exercises and readings which ask student writers to examine any subject with these strategic questions in mind and thus generate their own ideas on that subject. The authors also discuss the stages of inquiry that make up the problem-solving process (which includes the writing process) and procedures for developing argument and exposition that have as a goal "not skilled verbal coercion but discussion and exchange of ideas."

Christianity and Text

Father Walter Ong, in *"Maranatha:* Death and Life in the Text of the Book," [13] an essay in *Interfaces of the Word,* deals with the Bible as a "special case in the history of textuality," with special imperatives for modern Christians. "Interpretation of the Bible," he writes, "is for Christians more urgent than the interpretation of other texts. For the Christian believes that the Word of God is given in order to be interiorized, appropriated by men and women of all times and places." This imperative poses problems of Biblical interpretation: (1) written texts are a special kind of utterance in relation to time and the writer-reader relationship; (2) there is a distance between reader and listener, and between writer and speaker; (3) texts relate to other texts, providing literature, which is always of the past. Christians often resent these problems because the Bible seems open to a much simpler interpretation as a record of God speaking to man, addressed to all ages. Yet the relationship between the Word of God in the text of the Bible and the Word of God incarnate in Jesus has not been adequately defined.

After pointing up these problems, Ong asks four concluding questions concerning Biblical interpretation: (1) How far is the Bible to be considered a written composition and how far is it a record of God's actual speech, revealed to mankind? How far is the biblical message the participatory one of "pure orality" and how much the "analytic, explanatory" one of writing? (2) What are the implications for faith in the two processes, the oral and the written? (3) Can a reader of the Bible today also become a

listener? Should he? (4) What is the role of the Church in "resur-
recting the dead letter" into living speech?

In *Guardians of Tradition,* Ruth Elson[14] deals with the biblical
and Protestant orientations of nineteenth-century American
schoolbooks. She looks at over one thousand of the most popular
children's textbooks to study their social and cultural impact on
the child and also to identify what she calls the "lowest common
denominator of American intellectual history." She comes to the
conclusion that the nineteenth-century world of school books was
one of fantasy, with ideal villains and heroes and a benign Nature
perfectly planned by God for the good of man. Virtue would
always be rewarded and vice punished. The most fundamental assumption in these texts was that the universe was moral in character, that religion itself was a matter of morals rather than theology. The school books, through the last century took an un-
equivocal and monolithic stand on matters of basic morality.

Nature was regarded as serving man's purposes and as
having a mystical relationship with American freedom, which was
considered part of the American soil. The early Readers and
Spellers were devoted to the Bible and to God's relationship to
the universe and the child, but by the 1830s, the stories were no
longer biblical for the most part. The newer material stressed
death and God's punishment, argued against atheism and the
deism of Voltaire and Thomas Paine, and identified virtue with
Protestantism only (Catholics were depicted as a danger to the
state up to the 1870s).

There was no mention of some of the newer intellectual currents of the period—of Darwin's natural selection from chance
variation, of comparative religion, of literary realism, of William
James's pluralism. On the other hand the deeper realities of the
child's future life in a competitive world were faced head-on, with
admonitions about hardship, tragedy, devotion to a cause, and
the horrors of failure. On political questions, the United States
was presented as superior to all other nations, with a free society
autonomously developed, completely divorced from an international context; European culture was rejected as jaded and effete.
The social posture of these textbooks was consistently conservative, ignoring contemporary reform movements and offering a
vision of a serene, homogeneous America. Religious tolerance
was given lip-service but the implication was that recognizing
other religions as equal to Protestantism would subvert both
Church and State.

John McLeish looks back to an earlier merging of religion
and schooling in *Evangelical Religion and Popular Education.*[15] He

compares two evangelical movements as they developed in eighteenth-century Wales and early nineteenth-century England by focusing on their teaching the illiterate peasantry to read, an important by-product of their religious efforts. He concludes that religious enlightenment movements, when combined with adult literacy campaigns, take the form of social innovation; that mass illiteracy is perceived as a problem only when the society comes under the influence of more highly developed social organizations; that where mass illiteracy is confronted, change is due to deliberate acts of the intelligensia who are agents of enlightenment; and that Evangelical Christians call forth some of the best efforts for social change because they provide care, a sense of brotherhood, conscientiousness, and humane aspirations for the illiterate.

Modern Literacy Campaigns

Fidel Castro's effort to extend literacy in a revolutionary and secular context is described by Jonathan Kozol in "A New Look at the Literacy Campaign in Cuba." [16] In 1960 Castro announced that Cuba would, within a year, teach more than one million illiterate adult Cubans to read and write. Kozol's article, based on interviews and on Cuban publications, traces the history of the success of this Cuban campaign. He discusses the immense logistical and pedagogical challenges, the recruitment and training of the volunteer teachers, and the development in instructional methods that were openly political. About one hundred thousand young volunteers, 40 percent of whom were between the ages of ten and fourteen, answered the call to teach in the campaign.

There were, in his view, three basic elements motivating these volunteers: "ethical exhilaration" (exploding energy, rather than ideological compulsions); the charisma of Castro; and a massive organized effort coordinated through effective open propaganda. The campaign resulted in a transformation of one hundred thousand liberal, altruistic, and utopian young people into "a vanguard of committed or at least incipient socialists." These student volunteers were organized into military-style brigades who went through an eight- to ten-day training session on using teaching aids (a book of oral readings and a learner's primer), living and working in rural areas, and building solidarity by sharing in all the work. This training emphasis was designed to meet one of the explicit purposes of this campaign—to build a sense of solidarity between the urban and rural populations. The literacy campaign was "the seminal moment in their childhood formation as young socialists and active citizens of the newborn nation." No political indoctrination alone could have done this job.

The primer used in the campaign consisted of fifteen lessons presented as a story focusing on "active," emotive words, each preceded by a photograph of Cuban life, establishing a sense of equality and working in a common cause. The directives for teaching were uniformly sequenced—first, reading aloud and repeating sounds, then reading silently, then breaking down words into syllables. Teachers were to keep detailed diaries of their reactions, emotions, and errors and were urged to show respect toward the students who were willing to learn. Kozol comments that little of this style duplicates the rigid approach of Lenin's literacy campaigns, the North American missionary style devised by Frank Laubach, or the "mechanistic" methods of UNESCO. The approach is based on Friere's method developed in Brazil, in which there is a search for charged, active words and a relationship of dialogue between the teacher and the student, who chooses to be taught. The difference from Friere's method was that the Cuban reading material was more explicitly political and the teachers more directive.

By midsummer 1961, when more drastic measures were needed to fulfill Castro's promise, factory workers, revolutionary organizations, municipal education councils, and the National Congress were mobilized. By late 1961, less than 5 percent of Cuba's adult population remained illiterate, compared with 8 percent or more in every other Latin American country. The undisguised political character of the campaign called forth some heavy criticism from foreign observers, but Kozol defends such methods by arguing that all learning is ideological in some sense and it is praiseworthy that there has been "no other nation where the heroes and heroines of a revolution are so frequently the ones who fought with pen and primer, rather than solely those who fought with guns."

Frank Laubach has had a life-time of experience teaching illiterates in developing countries—25 years of work in 96 countries and 274 languages. *Toward World Literacy* [17] is his textbook of techniques "for liquidating illiteracy in any country—swiftly and completely." The methods, which are based in the missionary tradition, may now seem simplistic and the claims extravagant. But any reader can gain from Laubach's long experience as he describes the genesis of his methods, his teaching in both small villages and urban communities, and the teacher training and "how to" activities he promoted for graded readers and for making writing simple.

Sir Charles Jeffries is also concerned with tackling illiteracy on a world-wide basis. He attempts to outline, for the general reader, the problem of world illiteracy in the second half of the twentieth century.[18] Basing his examination on UNESCO information and other sources, he poses the problem that some 40 percent of the world's adult population—at least 700 million men and women—cannot read or write. He lists among the major difficulties the fact that functional literacy is the issue, rather than minimum literacy, that decisions must be based on language distribution and usage within any one country, and that educators have difficulty determining what is the most useful material to teach people. The contents of the book include an analysis of the problem, a review of pioneer attacks on illiteracy, midcentury experiences, UNESCO efforts, and the Teheran Conference. The volume also reviews reading materials that have been developed for new readers and their distribution. Jeffries concludes that illiteracy cannot be eliminated by expanding formal education because it is too expensive and requires a huge amount of organization and administration. He proposes an all-out effort "everywhere and at once." The emphasis should be on the basic skills, after which people can educate themselves, provided they have access to the proper literature. Ministries of literacy should be created in developing countries and literacy instructors, who need only to be of average ability and intelligence, should be trained. These activities could be funded through charitable sources, but the bulk of the support must come through government funding.

Literacy and Economic Development

Mark Blaug, in "Literacy and Economic Development," [19] concludes that the most we can say about the economic benefits of literacy is that "while literacy may not always cure poverty, affluence always eradicates illiteracy." So while it is not true that illiteracy is an absolute barrier to economic progress, it is true that there are definite limits to what an illiterate population can accomplish. Blaug further argues that since adult literacy has a quick pay-off, we are likely to see more expenditures targeted for adult education in the form of selective, intensive literacy campaigns. As to how much should be spent, we don't yet have enough experience with world-wide literacy campaigns to answer that question.

Blaug begins with the assumption that the objective of educational planning is to promote economic development, "subject to maintenance of national sovereignty and political stability." He claims that literacy benefits economic developments by raising the productivity of new literates and those working with them, reducing the costs of information transmittal, stimulating demand for vocational training, selecting out the most able and providing them occupational mobility, and strengthening economic incentives as rewards rise in response to new efforts. He adds that since school education takes six to eight years compared with one or two years of literacy training, the economic benefits of school education would have to be four or five times greater than those of adult literacy to produce identical cost/benefit ratios for the two types of learning.

In *Education and Economic Development,* edited by Anderson and Bowman,[20] Bowman looks at the relationship between development and literacy training. Anderson's article, "Literacy and Schooling on the Development Threshold," investigates the extent and distribution of literacy during the formative period of western industrial economies. From a historical comparison of levels of literacy, he concludes that about a 40 percent adult literacy level is a necessary threshold for economic development.

Can literacy by itself change attitudes and behavior? Inkeles, Schuman, and Smith, in their study of East Pakistan, "Some Social Psychological Effects and Non-Effects of Literacy in a New Nation," [21] relate literacy to a number of psychological characteristics of the common man participating in the economic and political development of his country. Much of their data comes from lengthy interviews with farmers and factory workers. They look at the extent to which measured literacy is associated with the level of education and verbal aptitude and discuss several ways in which literacy is and is not related to the development of new identities, perceptions, and attitudes. The authors argue that literacy opens the mind to new ideas that are not dependent on the immediate social situation, and that the literate man is quicker to perceive social change and can more easily redefine his beliefs to fit new needs.

A Postscript

Richard Hoggart in *The Uses of Literacy* [22] has raised questions about mass reading tastes in free literate societies. The changes in twentieth-century English society which have greatly increased the opportunity for education, he argues, have not arrested the trivialization of reading matter. Reading, which in other settings has promoted the intellectual growth of a people, now threatens to arrest it. The mass publications of sex, crime, and violence, he argues "make it harder for people without an intellectual bent to become wise in their own way."

It may seem surprising that Hoggart would be asking for wisdom in written discourse aimed at so broad an audience but then not so surprising when we remember that almost twenty-four hundred years ago Socrates made the same demand. In the *Phaedrus,* he set up a science of discourse that held written language, on any subject, to the highest standards of wisdom and truth.

> . . . complete lucidity and serious importance, he [the writer] will think, belong only to those lessons in justice and beauty and goodness which are delivered for the sake of true instruction and are, in fact inscribed in the soul. . . . [23]

Probably no author reviewed in this essay would disagree with Socrates's assertion that concerns about literacy are basically ethical and moral concerns.

Notes

1. Jack Goody and Ian Watt, "The consequences of Literacy," in *Literacy in Traditional Societies,* ed. J. Goody (Cambridge: Cambridge University Press, 1969), pp. 27–68.

2. David R. Olson, "From Utterance to Text: The Bias of Language in Speech and Writing," *Harvard Educational Review* 48 (1978): 341–77.

3. Patricia M. Greenfield, "Oral and Written Language: The Consequences for Cognitive Development in Africa, the United States and England," *Language and Speech* 15 (1972): 169–78.

4. Marshall McLuhan, *The Gutenberg Galaxy: The Making of Topographic Man* (Toronto: University of Toronto Press, 1962).

5. Walter J. Ong, S.J., *Interfaces of the Word: Studies in the Evolution of Consciousness and Culture* (Ithaca, New York: Cornell University Press, 1977).

6. Ortega Y Gasset, "The Difficulty of Reading," *Diogenes* 28 (1959): 1–17.

7. Basil Bernstein, "Social Class and Linguistic Development: A Theory of Social Learning," in *Education, Economy and Society, ed.* A. H. Halsey, et al. (New York: Free Press, 1961), pp. 288–314.

8. Doris R. Entwisle, "Implications of Language Socialization for Reading Models and for Learning to Read," *Reading Research Quarterly* (1970–71), pp. 111–67.

9. Michael Cole, J. Gay, J. Glick, and D. Sharp, *The Cultural Context of Learning and Thinking: An Exploration in Experimental Anthropology* (New York: Basic Books, 1971).

10. Jeanne Chall, *Learning to Read: The Great Debate: An Inquiry into the Science, Art, and Ideology of Old and New Methods of Teaching Children to Read, 1910–1965* (New York: McGraw-Hill, 1967).

11. Nan Elsasser, and Vera P. John-Steiner, "An Interactionist Approach to Advancing Literacy," *Harvard Educational Review* 47 (1972): 355–69.

12. Richard E. Young, Alton L. Becker, and Kenneth L. Pike, *Rhetoric: Discovery and Change* (New York: Harcourt, Brace, Jovanowich, Inc., 1970).

13. Walter J. Ong, S.J., *"Maranatha: Death and Life in the Text of the Book: The Bible as Text,"* in W. J. Ong, *Interfaces of the Word: Studies in the Evolution of Consciousness and Culture* (Ithaca: Cornell University Press, 1977).

14. Ruth M. Elson, *Guardians of Tradition: American Schoolbooks of the Nineteenth Century* (Lincoln: University of Nebraska, 1964).

15. John McLeish, *Envangelical Religion and Popular Education: A Modern Interpretation* (London: Methuen, 1969).

16. Jonathan Kozol, "A New Look at the Literacy Campaign in Cuba," *Harvard Educational Review* 48 (1978): 341–77.

17. Frank C. Laubach, and Robert S. Laubach, *Toward World Literacy, the Each One, Teach One Way* (Syracuse: Syracuse University Press, 1960).

18. Sir Charles Jeffries, *Illiteracy: A World Problem* (New York: F. A. Praeger, 1967).

19. Mark Blaug, "Literacy and Economic Development," *School Review* 74 (1966): 393–417.

20. C. A. Anderson and M. J. Bowman, eds., *Education and Economic Development* (Chicago: Aldine Publishing Co., 1963).

21. Alex Inkeles, Howard Schuman, and David H. Smith, "Some Social Psychological Effects and Non-Effects of Literacy in a New Nation," *Economic Development and Cultural Change* 16 (1967): 1–14.

22. Richard Hoggart, *The Uses of Literacy: Changing Patterns in English Mass Culture* (Harmondsworth: Pelican, 1958).

23. Plato, *Phaedrus,* trans. W. G. Helmbold and W. G. Rabinowitz (Indianapolis: Bobbs Merrill Educational Publishing, 1956), pp. 72–74.